HOMEMADE HEALTHY DOG FOOD COOKBOOK

A Guide to Healthier Eating for Your Canine
With 140 Delicious and Nutritious Homemade
Dog Food Recipes for a Happy and Satisfied Pet

Lucy Irving

TABLE OF CONTENTS

Introduction

Importance to Prepare Food for Your Dogs

Think about your diet. You might eat certain foods or recipes regularly, but you mix them up to avoid boredom and malnutrition. For example, food like beef jerky is delicious, but would you want to eat it for every meal? Store-bought dry dog food is dehydrated, baked, and condensed, which removes all the moisture content. Sound familiar? It's essentially the same process as drying out beef jerky.

Dried mainstream dog food offers a longer shelf life, but the methods used to produce huge batches of food remove many vital nutrients from the original ingredients. To make up for this loss of nutrients, pet food brands add powdered supplements to the food. These additions ensure the companies still hit the federally mandated minimum requirements necessary to claim their food is a complete and balanced meal for your dog.

Do you know what your dog is eating? By cooking for your dog, you know every single ingredient going into its body. That makes it easier to spot something that may not be right for it and adjust ingredients for its unique nutritional needs.

As it is well known, mass-produced dog food tends to have an incredible list of industrial components, including preservatives, so it will not be easy to identify exactly which ones have beneficial effects on your dog's health and which ones do not.

Now that you've decided to become a home chef for your dog, there will be no more running out of dog food and having to run out to the pet store before they close. You'll still have to get groceries, but chances are you're doing that anyway. Another huge bonus? Cooking the fresh and frozen ingredients in these recipes will add a good deal of moisture to your dog's meals. This is a great way to ensure your buddy gets all the water they need daily. Dogs can stop short of hydrating sufficiently. On days with big hikes, hot days, or highly active days, your dog is probably at the water bowl frequently. These days aside, the average dog sleeps 12 to 14 hours a day, so trips to the watering hole might not happen as much as they should.

For most people, pets are part of the family, and it is often a priority to create the best life possible for our furry friends. Home-cooked meals are just another way to give them what's best. Don't worry if cooking for your dog requires much time and effort. Just like preparing meals for yourself or your family, you'll fall into a rhythm quickly and be able to whip up simple recipes without a ton of effort. Once you determine which ingredients are supercharging your pup, you can adapt other recipes in the book to include impactful ingredients. The recipes are designed to give you the freedom to fit cooking for your dog into your life in the manner best for you.

Tips for Food Preparation and Storage

Preparing homemade dog food can be a great way to provide your furry friend with a nutritious and balanced diet. Here are some tips for food preparation and storage to ensure the safety and quality of homemade dog food:

- **Consult a veterinarian:** It is important to seek advice from a veterinarian before altering your dog's diet to ensure that homemade dog food is appropriate for your pet's requirements. They can guide you on the appropriate ingredients and portion sizes.
- **Use high-quality ingredients:** Select fresh, high-quality ingredients for your homemade dog food. Include a variety of lean meats (such as chicken, turkey, or beef), vegetables, and whole grains to provide a balanced diet. Steer clear of incorporating ingredients harmful to dogs, including onions, garlic, chocolate, grapes, and raisins.
- **Cook thoroughly:** To minimize the possibility of bacterial contamination, be sure to cook all meat and vegetables completely. Cooking also helps break down certain nutrients and makes them more digestible for dogs.
- **Avoid seasoning:** Dogs have sensitive digestive systems, and some common seasonings used in human food can be harmful to them. Avoid adding salt, spices, or flavor enhancers to your homemade dog food. Instead, focus on providing natural flavors through the ingredients you use.
- **Allow food to cool:** Before storing the homemade dog food, allow it to cool completely to room temperature. This helps prevent bacterial growth and condensation that can lead to spoilage.
- **Portion control:** Divide the cooked dog food into individual portions based on your dog's size, age, and activity level. Portion control helps ensure that your dog is getting the right amount of food and prevents overfeeding or underfeeding.
- **Refrigeration:** To preserve the homemade dog food, place it in tightly sealed containers and promptly refrigerate it. Cooling the food in the refrigerator helps inhibit the proliferation of bacteria. Label the containers with the date to keep track of freshness.
- **Freezing:** If you prepare a large batch of dog food, you can freeze individual portions for later use. Freezing helps extend the shelf life of homemade dog food. Use freezer-safe containers or resealable freezer bags, and again, don't forget to label them with the date.
- **Thawing:** When you're ready to serve frozen homemade dog food, thaw it in the refrigerator overnight. To prevent bacterial growth, refrain from thawing at room temperature. Thawed food should be used within a few days.
- **Monitor freshness:** Regularly check the stored homemade dog food for any signs of spoilage, such as an off odor, mold growth, or unusual texture. If you notice any abnormalities, discard the food and prepare a fresh batch.

Homemade Food Versus Industrial Food

Most pet owners want to ensure that their dogs have a long and happy life, and shifting to a homemade diet is an attempt to achieve that objective.

It was recently discovered in research conducted by the University of Guelph Ontario Veterinary College (UGOVC) in Canada that 87% of dog owners feed their canines human-grade food. Still, it's impossible to dismiss the importance of commercial dog food, routinely supplied since the mid-1800s by an industry.

Do you think homemade or store-bought dog food is better for your pup? Here's a short side-by-side comparison to aid your decision-making process.

Fresh Ingredients

Homemade dog food is unquestionably the best. To give your dog the freshest possible foods, you must make his meals yourself at home. The shelf life of most factory-made dog food is lengthy. Unsealed dry dog food may last up to 18 months; sealed canned food can last up to two years. Every time you buy a new bag or can of food, you should check the expiration date.

Fresh dog food delivery companies like The Farmer's Dog, which promises meals delivered within days after preparation, nonetheless have some lag time. It is best to begin preparing your dog food to offer your pet the freshest ingredients possible.

Nutritional Value

While you would assume that homemade dog food is superior to commercially produced kibble, this isn't necessarily true. Because dogs' dietary requirements and digestion vary from those of humans, homemade meals may be deficient in the beneficial components that dogs need. At the University of California–Davis Veterinary Medicine, a study examined 200 common dog food recipes and found 95 percent lacking in at least one vital vitamin.

In contrast, every dog food produced in the United States must fulfill USDA guidelines for balanced nutrition. The Center for Veterinary Medicine is the US Food and Drug Administration division that oversees ingredients. The implementation of state regulations governing the safe manufacturing and packaging of animal food is the responsibility of the Association of American Feed Control Officials.

Safety

As a result of several recalls in the previous 15 years, homemade dog food has become a growing trend. Around 180 pet food manufacturers voluntarily pulled their goods off the market in 2007 after reports surfaced that their products had caused renal damage or death in thousands of dogs and cats in the US and Canada.

Commercial dog food isn't the only source of foodborne disease. Only 2% of recorded foodborne disease incidents in 2010 were linked to pet food, according to 2010 research. That's compared to the 76 million instances of foodborne disease globally each year, which result in approximately 5,000 deaths.

You should also be aware of typical foods that might be unhealthy or deadly to dogs while preparing meals. Avocado, chocolate, grapes, and raisins are all on the shortlist.

The Benefits of Homemade Dog Food

Having complete control over what is put into your dog's body can be an eye-opening experience, and you will notice the changes that a new diet will bring to your dog, all of which will surely prompt you to take better care of yourself.

Fresh and Healthy Ingredients

Most of us are aware that fresh and nutrient-rich ingredients are the key to a healthy eating regime. You wouldn't put diesel fuel in a race car and expect the same speed and performance as it would get with the high-octane fuel it was built to run on. That's true for the fuel we put into our dogs, too. Each breed, mix, and individual is unique, and each dog's lifestyle is also unique. Taking the time to ensure they have the nutrients their bodies were built to process benefits everything from their energy level to their bladder and immune system function.

No Fillers, Weird Processing of Animal Parts, or Added Dyes

Manufactured dog food has come a long way in the last decade. Some of the products people have paid money for as pet food over the years would send chills down your spine: rotten meat, plastics, and Styrofoam, for example. But plenty of unsavory ingredients are still going into today's store-bought canine formulas. When manufacturing dog food, companies are held to a lower set of rules and standards than our food must meet. These "feed grade" standards are deemed suitable for animals but not humans. These guidelines and regulations allow some nasty ingredients, such as fillers, processed animal parts, and dyes, to slip through the cracks.

Control for Food Allergies

A huge advantage to making your dog food yourself is being able to see how different ingredients affect your dog. If you notice the dog is more energetic after a certain protein, veggie, or another ingredient, you can adapt the recipes around that food choice. Alternatively, if you notice something is slowing the dog down or the food does not seem to be the fuel they need, you can cut it out and adapt the recipes away from that particular ingredient. Cooking meals for your dog can also help control allergies and allows you to make small changes to their diet. This control can help keep the dog from forming new allergies. If a dog gets the same nourishment every day, the chances of developing allergies to that meal increase, and because many manufactured foods are similar in formula, the allergen could be present in many store-bought choices.

Improved Skin, Coat, and Overall Health

When dogs get a properly balanced diet, you can see it all over them. Different ingredients are suitable for different needs. For example, adding the right amount of omega-3 and omega-6 fatty acids are good for a dog's joints and shows in its silky coat. The proper ratio is about four parts omega-6s to one-part omega-3s. Eggs are also beneficial to their coat. A proper dose of fatty acids and added exercise typically improve joint health, bones, coats, and muscle growth.

Variety of Meals

Everyone enjoys and benefits from a little variety in their diet, but when it comes to your pup, a proper transition time is important. If done too abruptly, your dog's diet changes can result in gas, diarrhea, or an upset stomach. In my view, the benefits of variety outweigh the difficulty of transitioning between foods. All it takes is a bit of forethought to switch foods with little to no abdominal discomfort to your dog.

The recipes in this book lend themselves to easy food transitions, as they are designed so that you can make small substitutions while cooking them. For example, use ground turkey in a ground beef recipe for a day or two before switching to a week or two of turkey recipes. This process will allow the dog to easily digest the bulk of the ingredients they've grown accustomed to eating, and they will only have to form new bacteria to digest the protein change. Small changes always give the body a better chance of adapting.

Your Dog's Joy

Your dog is going to love this new diet. They can smell and taste every ingredient separately. You don't have to set their bowl up to look like a three-course meal. If you mix ingredients, the dog's senses are advanced enough to enjoy each flavor.

Homemade Is Budget Friendly

If your dog has an allergy, you can spend vast amounts of time researching foods and testing different ingredients and run up huge vet bills. You also have to factor in the cost of buying new dog foods to try. Suppose you can start to feel like you are chasing your tail. Home cooking will allow you to avoid potential allergies by rotating your dog's meals. If your dog has an allergy, these recipes will make it easier to determine what they are allergic to since the list of ingredients is so much shorter.

- The average cost of quality canned dog food is just over $3 per pound.
- The average cost of quality dry dog food ranges between $2 and $3 per pound.
- The average cost of high-quality fresh store-bought dog food is around $6.50 per pound.

The per lb cost of homemade dog food will also be around $6 or $7. However, the more you buy, the more you save. If you have the room, you can buy in bulk and get the cost down even lower.

Understanding Homemade Dog Food Diets

Types of Homemade Dog Food Diets

When it comes to feeding a homemade diet, four popular options are available right now. The most popular or at least the most talked about option is the "raw diet." This alternative focuses on providing unprocessed raw meats and, in some cases, fruits and veggies.

Another option is called the BARF Diet. This one is based on an "ancestral" diet and is focused on the idea that dogs are omnivores. It uses unprocessed and "biologically appropriate" foods such as meat, bones, organs, fruits, vegetables, and supplements.

The Prey Model Raw (PMR) Diet is a third option. It is an animal-exclusive diet that focuses on what dogs would typically eat in the wild. The ingredients focus on meat, bones, organs, and feathers and don't have any fruits and vegetables.

Lastly, there is the DIY Homemade Dog Food Diet. This is a whatever-works diet with no specific rules other than what works for your pet and provides them with the adequate nutrition they need. There is no inclusion or exclusion of specific foods. Unlike the raw food models, these diets can include both cooked and uncooked foods and appropriate supplements.

This last option is often the most preferred of those in the pet industry. This is because it allows the pet owner to design completely nutritional recipes and meals and doesn't place any unreasonable rules or restrictions that may hinder a pet owner from creating a diet. This brings up the question of whether creating homemade food for your dog is right for you.

Comparison of Homemade Dog Food Diets

Are home-cooked meals for your dog less costly than buying them? The answer is that it is probably not. Below are some things to remember:

- **Budget:** From $1/lb for dry kibble to over $20 for a 13-oz dog food container, costs may vary widely in the retail market. Calculate your current meal costs to understand how much it will cost to make a move.
- **Ingredients:** What will you need to make your dog food if you decide to do so? Do you know how much they cost and whether they're accessible in your neighborhood? Although duck is often used in homemade dishes since it's cheaper than chicken and easier to get year-round, it's not always available.
- **Effort and time:** What is the value of your time? Buying dog food at the store is a no-brainer. Open the bag and take out the appropriate quantity to serve. In comparison, making your dog food requires more time and work. Cooking and storing meals effectively takes more than just purchasing the necessary components.

When deciding whether to give your dog store-bought or handmade food, you should take into account many points. Considering his age, health, and lifestyle, as well as your money and availability, is essential.

Carry out your research and discuss it with your veterinarian before making any decisions. Because of their extensive knowledge of canine health, they can help make informed choices about how to best care for your pet. Working together, you can feel confident that your dog gets the best diet possible for its health, happiness, and long-term well-being.

Security Issues to Keep in Mind

When making homemade healthy dog foods, it's important to consider several security issues to ensure your pet's well-being.

Nutritional Balance

Dogs require a balanced diet to thrive. Seek guidance from a veterinarian or a specialist in veterinary nutrition to gain insights into the distinctive dietary requirements of your canine companion.

Ensure that the homemade meals provide the necessary nutrients, including proteins, carbohydrates, fats, vitamins, and minerals, in the correct proportions.

Allergies & Sensitivities

Just like humans, dogs can have food allergies or sensitivities. Be aware of any ingredients that your dog may be allergic to, such as certain proteins or grains, and avoid using them in homemade recipes.

Quality of Ingredients

Choose high-quality ingredients for your dog's food. Use fresh, human-grade meats, vegetables, and grains to minimize the risk of bacterial contamination or exposure to harmful substances.

Avoid using ingredients that could prove toxic to dogs, such as onions, garlic, chocolate, grapes, and sultanas.

Safe Food Handling

Practice proper food safety and hygiene when preparing homemade dog food. Wash your hands thoroughly before and after handling ingredients. Clean and disinfect all utensils, cutting boards, and surfaces to prevent cross-contamination. Ensure the meat is thoroughly cooked to eliminate any possible harmful microorganisms.

Storage and Shelf Life

Store homemade dog food properly to maintain its freshness and prevent spoilage. Refrigerate or freeze the food in airtight containers to inhibit bacterial growth. Follow recommended storage guidelines and avoid keeping the food longer than the recommended duration.

Transitioning and Monitoring

When introducing homemade food to your dog's diet, do it gradually to allow their digestive system to adjust. Monitor your dog's response to the new diet, including their appetite, energy levels, and overall well-being. In case you observe any negative reactions or have any concerns, it is advisable to seek advice from your veterinarian.

Professional Guidance

It's always beneficial to seek guidance from a veterinarian or a veterinary nutritionist when preparing homemade dog food. They can provide you with personalized advice, ensure that the diet meets your dog's specific needs, and address any concerns or questions you may have.

Essentials of Homemade Dog Food

Key Ingredients

When it comes to making a recipe for your dog, you should follow some guidelines. For example, you should use a single type of food, such as chicken, to make up more than half of the diet. Unless specified, homemade dog food recipes can be either raw or cooked. Human food leftovers can be included as long as they are safe human foods. Let's look at some of the guidelines to follow when creating your dog food recipes.

Meat and Animal Products

These should always make up at least half of the diet. Raw diets for dogs can be high in fat, which leads to obesity. Another hazard of diets too high in fat is that when restricting how much a dog is given to control weight, the dog may develop a deficiency for some required nutrients. Unless you provide your dog with regular, intense exercise, then you should use lean meats with no more than ten percent fat, remove the skin from poultry, and cut off any separable fat. It is best to feed dark meat poultry rather than breast meat; unless your dog needs a very low-fat diet.

Raw Meaty Bones

These are optional, but if you feed them, they should only make up one-third to one-half of the dog's total diet. If you feed bony parts like chicken necks and back, you should trend to the lower end of the range. If you use the meatier parts like the thighs, you can use more. You should also never feed cooked bones.

Boneless Meat

It is best to include both red meat and poultry. A good choice is a heart since it is lean and less expensive to purchase than other muscle meats.

Fish

This is a good source of Vitamin D, which needs to be supplemented. Some good choices are canned fish with bones like sardines, jack mackerel, and pink salmon. You should remove the bones from the fish you cook yourself and never feed your dog raw fish. You can feed small amounts of fish each day, or you can feed it in larger amounts once or twice a week. The total amount you feed shouldn't exceed 1oz of fish per pound of other meats.

Organs

Approximately five percent of this group should consist of liver, which equates to around one ounce of liver per pound of other animal products. The most nutritious option is beef liver, but you should also include other liver types occasionally. You should feed small amounts of liver each day or every other day rather than feed a larger portion less often.

Eggs

These are a highly nutritious addition to any diet. Dogs who weigh about twenty lb can have a whole egg each day, but smaller dogs should get less.

Dairy

Most dogs tolerate plain yogurt and kefir well. Some other good options are cottage and ricotta cheeses. However, you should limit other cheese forms since they are high in fat.

Fruits and Vegetables

These don't play a large role in the dog's evolutionary diet. However, fruits and vegetables provide fiber that helps support digestive health, antioxidants, and other valuable nutrients that can help improve the health and length of a dog's life. The most nutritious options are deeply colored vegetables and fruits.

Starchy Vegetables

Vegetables such as potatoes, sweet potatoes, winter squashes, and legumes provide carbohydrate calories that can help reduce the cost of a homemade food diet while keeping weight on underweight and/or highly active dogs. For overweight dogs, the quantities should be limited. To be digestible, you need to cook starchy vegetables.

Non-Starchy and Leafy Green Vegetables

These vegetables are low in calories and can be added to any amount you want. Just keep in mind that too much of these vegetables can cause gas. In addition, raw, cruciferous vegetables such as broccoli and cauliflower can intentionally suppress thyroid function. Raw vegetables must be pureed in a food processor, blender, or juicer so that dogs can digest them properly. Whole raw vegetables aren't harmful and can even be fed as treats.

Fruits

The best choices for this are bananas, apples, berries, melon, and papaya. However, you should avoid raisins and grapes, which can lead to kidney failure.

Grains

This category is controversial since it can cause inflammation due to allergies, arthritis, or inflammatory bowel disease (IBD). Some grains also contain gluten which can cause digestive problems in some dogs. Most dogs will do fine with grains, which can help reduce the cost of feeding a homemade diet.

Grains and starchy vegetables shouldn't make up any more than half a diet. Some good grain choices are oatmeal, brown rice, quinoa, barley, and pasta. You can use white rice to settle an upset stomach. However, white rice is low in nutrition and shouldn't make up a large portion of the diet. Ensure all grains you use are well cooked.

Key Nutrients

- **Carbohydrates.** They are a dog's primary fuel source and must be part of its daily diet because they give the dog glucose, a form of energy. They also contain a lot of dietary fiber, which is good for your dog.
- **Proteins.** The muscular meat of a variety of animals should be the primary source of protein your dog consumes regularly. It's also important to get some of your dog's protein from organic meat, even if it's just a little bit.
- **Fats.** They promote a healthy nervous system, give your dog energy, and regulate its body temperature. However, not all fats are good for your dog. Ensure you choose a healthy, quality source of fats for your pet.
- **Water.** It is essential to take the necessary steps to ensure your dog has everyday access to an adequate supply of clean water. Water is essential to a dog's health and well-being.
- **Vitamins.** They are responsible for a wide range of different functions in a dog's body. Dogs shouldn't consume too much or too little of it. There should be a balance to avoid complications.
- **Fiber.** Dogs should get enough fiber as it is great for their digestive systems. The fermentation of fiber in a dog's intestinal tract typically produces fatty acids, which in turn helps prevent the excessive growth of intestinal bacteria.
- **Fruits and Vegetables.** Fruits and vegetables provide dogs with the same benefits they provide for humans. However, they can't eat some fruits. Make sure to consult with your vet for guidance.
- **Minerals.** They are responsible for a wide variety of processes within a dog, including forming bones and maintaining their strength.

Kitchen Utensils and Equipment You'll Need

You'll need some basic kitchen tools to cook these recipes, but if you are equipped to cook basic meals for yourself already, you've probably got most of the necessary tools.

Cutting Board

Cutting boards come in handy for all your cooking. I like flexible, colored cutting boards because I can color code to avoid cross-contamination (for example, red for meats and green for veggies). They also make transferring chopped food into a pan or a bowl a breeze.

Fine Mesh Strainer

A fine mesh strainer is perfect for rinsing quinoa or rice and draining fat from meat. I prefer one that hangs over the sink, providing a very controlled scenario when pouring scalding water into the sink.

Ice Cube Trays

These are perfect for bite-size frozen treats. I recommend silicone trays, as they make it very easy to remove frozen treats without breaking their form. Silicone trays come in a variety of sizes and fun shapes.

Immersion Blender or Food Processor

I like an immersion blender when it comes to processing food. It's smaller, more versatile, and easier to clean than a food processor. A food processor gets the job done and can be very helpful, especially if you are cooking larger amounts. No need for both; either one will do.

Kitchen Knives (High Quality)

High-quality kitchen knives make a huge difference but can cost a fortune. However, an entire set isn't the only way—you can build as you go. Get the feel of a weighted, razor-sharp, high-quality knife, and you will realize how much effort and time you've wasted with dull knives.

Multicookers

I recommend a stockpot with a steamer basket attachment. These are sometimes pasta pots or multicookers (not to be confused with pressure cookers or instant pots). This pot allows you to steam veggies over rice. The upside is that nutrients that tend to cook out of the veggies drip right into the rice. It will also come with a strainer lid for draining pasta. Fewer pots mean less cleanup, and that's always good!

Nested Mixing Bowls

A set of nested mixing bowls is always helpful. They stack neatly into each other for space-saving storage. Get a set with lids, and they can double as storage containers.

Nonstick Baking Sheets

Many of the treats require a baking sheet. Size and variety will depend on your needs; any of them will work for baking the dog treats.

Pots and Pans

A good set of nonstick or stainless-steel pots and pans is essential for any kitchen. You will likely use them every day for years. If cared for, they could be the only set you ever buy. There are many different options, so if you don't already own a set, find the style that suits you the best.

Roasting Pan

A roasting pan is nice, but other baking pans have racks to keep meat and bones out of drippings and fat, and they will serve the same purpose. Find the size that's right for you.

Rolling Pin

The treat recipes require making a dough that needs to be rolled flat. Different materials and styles are available—whichever one allows you to roll dough flat is the right choice.

Stand Mixer or Hand Mixer

All the treat recipes call for a mixer; even a couple of the main courses use the stand mixer to shred pulled chicken. A hand mixer will work, too, so if that's what you've got, you can make do. A stand mixer is another tool that, if cared for, will last forever. They come in handy for many recipes, and there are attachments to transform them into a machine suitable for various types of specialty cooking.

Steamer Basket

Steaming vegetables is a good way to keep their nutrients from cooking out. Boiling vegetables tends to remove many of the nutrients, so steaming is a better option. If you have a multicooker, use the attached steamer basket. You can also buy one on its own.

Stockpot

Stockpots are ideal for large portions; there's plenty of room to simmer many ingredients and keep the splattering or splashing contained in the deep walls. Look for one with a heavy bottom for the best results.

Storage Containers

A set of airtight containers is probably something you already have since some meals keep improving as leftovers. You'll want several different container sizes to suit your needs.

Utensils

A wooden spoon, spatula, and rice paddle are all helpful. These are the tools you'll use every time you cook, regardless of what you cook, so these utensils are a must.

Prepare Homemade Dog Food Safely

A few things should never be given to a dog to eat. Some meals are safe and suitable for human consumption but can be fatal for our dogs. We shouldn't give these meals to our dogs. Below is a list of things dogs can't eat:

- **Potato peels.** Throw away any parts of the potato that have turned green or sprouted. This applies to all kinds of potatoes.
- **Cherries.** Cherries have a potential health risk due to cyanide in the fruit's stems, leaves, and pits. Although, occasionally, your dog can enjoy a couple of cherries that have been destemmed and seeded without any problems.
- **Caffeine.** Caffeine causes irregular heartbeats in dogs, which can be dangerous. In addition to this, it is also capable of causing convulsions and tremors.

- **Alliums.** Any member of the allium family, when consumed in large quantities, has the potential to be harmful. However, extremely non-frequent use of a tiny portion is allowed. The allium family includes onions, garlic, and leeks, among others.
- **Raw yeast dough**. Raw yeast dough can cause bellyache and bloat.
- **Rhubarb leaves.** The rhubarb leaves are harmful, but the stems are not and can be helpful for dogs that suffer from constipation.
- **Chocolate.** Theobromine can be found in chocolate. Your dog will most likely experience nothing more serious than an upset stomach if the amount given to them is low. But when consumed in large quantities, theobromine can cause internal bleeding, tremors, and seizures. Steer clear of sugar-free chocolate also, as they contain artificial sweeteners and can cause more harm to your dog.
- **Xylitol.** It is highly toxic to dogs. This particular artificial sweetener causes insulin levels to rise.
- **Ice Cream.** Some dairy products, like milk, can be difficult for dogs to digest.
- **Alcohol.**
- **Nutmeg.**
- **Avocado.**
- **Macadamia Nuts.**
- **Grapes and Raisins.**

Additional Tips and Resources on Homemade Dog Food

How to Store Homemade Dog Food

When storing homemade dog food, following proper food safety guidelines is essential to ensure that the food remains fresh and safe for your dog to consume. Here are some tips on this process:

- **Allow the food to cool:** Before storing homemade dog food, let it cool completely. This helps prevent bacterial growth and condensation inside the storage container.
- **Choose appropriate containers:** Use airtight containers or storage bags specifically designed for storing food. Glass or BPA-free plastic containers with tight-fitting lids are good options. Make sure the containers are clean and dry before use.
- **Portion the food:** Divide the homemade dog food into individual portions based on your dog's serving size. This makes it easier to thaw and feed later without exposing the entire batch to air and potential contamination.
- **Label and date:** Label each container with the preparation date and the food type. This ensures you can keep track of the freshness and rotation of the dog food.
- **Refrigeration:** If you plan to use homemade dog food within a few days, store it in the refrigerator. Keep the containers on the lower shelves to minimize temperature fluctuations. Ideally, use the food within 3-4 days to maintain its freshness and quality.
- **Freezing:** If you're making a larger batch or want to store the food longer, freezing is the best option. Ensure that the food is completely cooled before freezing it. Place the individual portions in freezer-safe containers or storage bags, removing as much air as possible to prevent freezer burn. Using the food within 2-3 months is recommended for optimal taste and nutritional value.
- **Thawing:** When feeding your dog, thaw the frozen homemade dog food in the refrigerator overnight or use the defrost setting on your microwave. Avoid thawing at room temperature, as it can promote bacterial growth.
- **Serving:** Serve the homemade dog food in clean bowls or dishes. Discard any uneaten portions after a reasonable amount of time to prevent spoilage.

Your Dog's Transition to a Homemade Diet

Transitioning your dog from one food to another shouldn't be done without a conversation with your veterinarian. Make an appointment and talk with the doctor about the dietary change you would like to make and your reasons behind it. Using your dog's current health status and weight along with past veterinary records, your veterinarian can help you devise a home-cooked diet with complete meals that covers all the bases of the nutritional levels for your dog.

If your veterinarian is uncertain about fresh food contents and levels, ask for a referral to a board-certified veterinary nutritionist who can develop a diet that is best for your pup. The doctor can tell you want your dog needs nutritionally in terms of age, weight, and breed. Remember that you always have this book as a guide, but it's not a substitute for your veterinarian's medical knowledge about your dog.

Don't leave the appointment without having all your questions to the veterinarian answered clearly and thoroughly.

When your veterinarian gives you the go-ahead, and after you have purchased your ingredients, try some recipes printed here. All the meals in this book are designed to be easy to make, highly nutritious, and low-fat. When it's time to consider switching your dog from its old food to the new fresh diet, gradually change your dog's regimen. Too abrupt a change can cause some unpleasant stomach upset for your pup, including vomiting, diarrhea, and gas.

When making the change, follow these steps to switch your dog over to the home-cooked die slowly:

Gradually Mix the Food

Gradually mix the food by adding a small amount of the new food while slightly reducing the old food; use a 25% new / 75% old ratio to start. Over the next 7 - 10 days, slowly alter the food proportions to a 50% / 50% ratio, then 75% / 25%, and finally, switch your pup to the new diet entirely.

Keep an Eye Out for an Upset Stomach

Keep an eye out for an upset stomach which can happen during this process even if you are placing your dog on a higher-quality diet. Your dog should drink its usual amount of water, shouldn't have too much gas, and the poop should be firm, not runny. Remember to be patient with your dog if having accidents as its body is adjusting to the new food.

Slow Things Down Even Further

Slow things down even further if you see any uncharacteristic behavior from your dog, such as lethargy or depression. Contact your veterinarian for their input on your dog's health status.

Don't Get Discouraged

Don't get discouraged if your dog doesn't take to the new food immediately. Although it's rare, as most dogs will quickly be swayed by the natural smells of fresh dog food, some dogs might turn up their noses at first. They are so used to the kibble they've eaten for years that alternatives seem scary. With time, your dog will happily leap into fresh, natural food.

Common Mistakes When Feeding Homemade Dog Food

Feeding homemade dog food can be a great way to ensure your furry friend receives a nutritious and balanced diet. However, people make a few common mistakes when preparing homemade dog food. Here are a few to avoid:

Nutritional Imbalance

One of the most significant mistakes is failing to provide a balanced diet. Dogs require a specific balance of proteins, carbohydrates, fats, vitamins, and minerals. Your dog may suffer from deficiencies or other health issues if you don't include all the necessary nutrients. Consult a veterinarian or a veterinary nutritionist to develop a balanced recipe.

Insufficient Protein

Dogs are primarily carnivorous animals and require adequate protein in their diet. Ensure to include high-quality protein sources like lean meats (chicken, beef, turkey), fish, or eggs. Insufficient protein can lead to muscle wasting and other health problems.

Inappropriate Ingredients

It has been mentioned some foods safe for humans can be harmful or toxic to dogs. Avoid onions, garlic, grapes, raisins, chocolate, caffeine, alcohol, and artificial sweeteners (xylitol). These can cause severe health issues or even be fatal for dogs.

Lack of Variety

Providing a variety of foods is essential to meet your dog's nutritional needs. Don't rely solely on one or two ingredients. Incorporate a mix of meats, vegetables, and grains to ensure a well-rounded diet.

Poor Food Preparation

Proper food handling and preparation are vital to avoid foodborne illnesses. Make sure to wash your hands, utensils, and cooking surfaces thoroughly. Prevent cross-contamination by ensuring that raw meat is kept separate from other ingredients.

Overfeeding or Underfeeding

Accurate portion control is crucial when feeding homemade dog food. Obesity can result from excessive food intake, whereas malnutrition can arise from insufficient food consumption. Seek guidance from your veterinarian to establish the suitable proportions of food for your dog, considering their age, size, activity level, & general well-being.

Lack of Calcium

Dogs require a sufficient amount of calcium for healthy bones and teeth. If you're not feeding commercial dog food, it's important to include a calcium source in your homemade dog food. Consult your veterinarian for recommendations on appropriate calcium supplementation.

Ignoring Food Allergies or Sensitivities

Just like humans, dogs can have food allergies or sensitivities. Pay attention to any adverse reactions your dog may have to certain ingredients and adjust the recipe accordingly. Common dog allergens include grains (such as wheat or corn) and certain proteins (like beef or chicken).

Before embarking on this culinary journey for your beloved furry friend, I would love to hear your opinion. But first, let's take a moment to savor the anticipation of preparing a homemade dish that is not only delicious but also filled with love and nourishment for your dog.

Are you excited to whip up a dish that will make your friend wag their tail, aren't you? I can't wait to hear about your experience with these recipes. After trying your first homemade dish, I invite you to leave a review on Amazon. Your feedback is like a flavorful seasoning that enhances the taste of this cookbook!

Homemade Recipes for Puppy

Chicken Cauliflower Carrot Stir-Fry

Preparation time: 5 minutes

Cooking time: 15 minutes

Servings: 2

Ingredients:

- ½ cup cauliflower florets
- ½ cup chicken, minced
- 2 Jalapeno, chopped
- 1 carrot, chopped
- ⅓ tsp cinnamon
- ⅓ tsp basil powder
- 1 leek, sliced
- 1 tsp peanut oil
- 2 tbsp water

Directions:

1. Add the cauliflower florets to a blender.
2. Pulse them until they are grainy. In a large skillet, add the peanut oil.
3. Fry the chicken until slightly brown.
4. Add the carrot, cauliflower, and leek. Stir for 3 minutes.
5. Add the cinnamon, basil powder, and jalapeno. Stir for 2 minutes.
6. Add 2 tablespoons of water and cover with a lid.
7. Cook on medium-low heat for 5 minutes. Serve.

Nutrition per serving: Calories: 250 kcal; Fat: 8 g; Carbs: 15 g; Protein: 25 g

Squash With Chicken and Basil

Preparation time: 5 minutes

Cooking time: 15 minutes

Servings: 2

Ingredients:

- 2 chicken breasts, chopped
- ¼ cup basil leaves
- ½ cup chopped squash
- ¼ tsp cinnamon
- ¼ tsp turmeric
- ½ tsp olive oil

Directions:

1. Heat the olive oil in a pan.
2. Fry the chicken for 2 minutes.
3. Add the squash, then stir for 3 minutes.
4. Add the basil, cinnamon, and turmeric, then stir for 4 minutes.
5. Serve.

Nutrition per serving: Calories: 255 kcal; Fat: 8 g; Carbs: 6 g; Protein: 41 g

Chicken Veggie Risotto

Preparation time: 5 minutes

Cooking time: 15 minutes

Servings: 2

Ingredients:

- ½ cup chicken breast, shredded
- 1 carrot, chopped roughly
- 1 green bell pepper, chopped
- 1 tbsp leek, chopped
- ½ cup rice
- 1 cup chicken broth
- 1 tsp sesame oil
- ½ tsp cinnamon

Directions:

1. In a huge skillet, add the sesame oil.
2. Add the chicken and toss for 2 minutes.
3. Add the leek, rice and stir for 2 minutes.

4. Add cinnamon and chicken broth and cook for 8 minutes.
5. Add the bell pepper and carrot.
6. Cook for 5 minutes. Serve.

Nutrition per serving: Calories: 179 kcal; Fat: 4.3 g; Carbs: 20.8 g; Protein: 14.9 g

Chicken Couscous

Preparation time: 5 minutes

Cooking time: 15 minutes

Servings: 2

Ingredients:

- ⅓ cup couscous
- ½ cup chicken cubes
- ¼ cup peas
- 1 tbsp coriander leaves, chopped
- ½ tsp turmeric
- ½ tsp cumin
- ½ tsp olive oil
- ⅓ tsp cinnamon
- ½ cup water

Directions:

1. Heat the olive oil in a pot.
2. Add the chicken and fry until golden.
3. Mix in the couscous and stir for 1 minute.
4. Add the cinnamon, turmeric, and cumin, then stir for 3 minutes.
5. Pour in ½ cup water. Cook for 5 minutes on high heat.
6. Add the peas and cook for another 3 minutes.
7. Place the coriander leaves on top and serve.

Nutrition per serving: Calories: 290 kcal; Fat: 6 g; Carbs: 34 g; Protein: 24 g

Oat Yogurt Cookies

Preparation time: 5 minutes

Cooking time: 25 minutes

Servings: 50 treats

Ingredients:

- 1 cup Greek yogurt
- 1 ½ cup oats
- 2 eggs
- 1 cup cheese, shredded
- 2 tbsp beef broth
- 2 cups wheat flour

Directions:

1. Beat the eggs in a bowl.
2. Add the cheese and mix well.
3. Add in the yogurt and mix again.
4. Add the beef broth, and mix.
5. Then, add the oats and wheat flour. Fold in gently.
6. Make the dough, then let it rest in the fridge for 10 minutes.
7. Roll it out and cut it into bone shapes.
8. Add to a cookie sheet. Bake for 15 minutes.

Nutrition per serving: Calories: 80 kcal; Fat: 2.5 g; Carbs: 10 g; Protein: 4 g

Baked Oat Veggie Treats

Preparation time: 5 minutes

Cooking time: 15 minutes

Servings: 6

Ingredients:

- 2 eggs
- 1 cup oats
- 1 carrot, shredded
- 10 basil leaves, chopped
- ½ tsp turmeric
- ½ tsp cinnamon
- ⅓ tsp cumin

Directions:

1. Grease a muffin tray using oil.
2. In a mixing bowl, beat the eggs.
3. Add the turmeric, cinnamon, and cumin.
4. Add the oats, carrots, and basil. Mix well.
5. Add the mixture to the muffin tray. Spread the top evenly.
6. Bake for 15 minutes. Serve.

Nutrition per serving: Calories: 112 kcal; Fat: 4 g; Carbs: 13 g; Protein: 6 g

Liver Training Treats

Preparation time: 20 minutes

Cooking time: 40 minutes

Servings: 45 training treats

Ingredients:

- 2 cups whole-wheat flour
- 1 lb raw organic beef liver, rinsed
- ½ cup water
- 1 egg

Directions:

1. Preheat your oven to 350°F.
2. Add the liver to a food processor and puree until smooth.
3. Transfer the pureed liver to a bowl and add egg, flour, and water. Mix well. Grease a cookie sheet and pour batter onto it.
4. Place it in the oven and bake for 25-30 minutes. Retrieve the cookie sheet from the oven. Score the treats into squares about ½ inch.
5. Return the cookie sheet to the oven for about 7-10 minutes to dry the treats completely. Turn off the oven, retrieve the cookie sheet, and flip the treats. Then, return the cookie sheet to the cooling oven. Let the treats remain in the oven until it cools completely.

6. Keep it in the refrigerator for 3 days or store it in a sealed container in the freezer for up to 6 months.

Nutrition per serving: Calories: 20 kcal; Fat: 0.5 g; Carbs: 3 g; Protein: 1 g

Corn Dog Muffin

Preparation time: 5 minutes

Cooking time: 15 minutes

Servings: 6

Ingredients:

- 2 sausages, cut into 6 pieces
- ½ cup wheat flour
- ½ cup cornmeal
- 1 egg
- 1 tsp baking powder
- 2 tbsp almond milk
- ½ tsp cumin
- ⅓ tsp turmeric
- 1 tbsp almond butter, melted

Directions:

1. Beat the egg in a bowl.
2. Add muffin liners to a muffin tray.
3. Add the almond butter and almond milk to the egg.
4. Add the cornmeal and wheat flour.
5. Mix in the baking powder, cumin, and turmeric.
6. Fold into a smooth batter.
7. Pour the mixture into the muffin tray. Add one piece of sausage to each muffin.
8. Bake for 15 minutes. Serve.

Nutrition per serving: Calories: 210 kcal; Fat: 11 g; Carbs: 20 g; Protein: 8 g

Peanut Butter Apple Muffin

Preparation time: 5 minutes

Cooking time: 15 minutes

Servings: 6

Ingredients:

- 1 egg
- 1 cup wheat flour
- 2 tbsp almond milk
- 2 tbsp almond butter
- 1 tsp baking powder
- ½ cup apple puree
- ½ tsp cinnamon powder
- • 2 tbsp peanut butter

Directions:

1. Beat the egg in a bowl.
2. Add the almond butter and peanut butter and mix well.
3. Add the apple puree, and almond milk, then mix.
4. Sift in the dry ingredients. Fold in gently.
5. Add muffin liners to the muffin tray.
6. Pour in the batter. Tap twice and bake for 15 minutes. Serve.

Nutrition per serving: Calories: 180 kcal; Fat: 7 g; Carbs: 24 g; Protein: 5 g

Fruity Yogurt Puppy Parfait

Preparation time: 15 minutes

Cooking time: 0 minutes

Servings: Approximately 16 lb

Ingredients:

- ½ cup plain yogurt
- ½ cup fresh strawberries (chopped)
- ½ cup fresh blueberries (chopped)
- ½ cup applesauce

Directions:

1. Add all ingredients to a bowl and stir until well blended.
2. Serve a little of the parfait at a time to avoid overfeeding.

Nutrition per serving: Calories: 30 kcal; Fat: 0.2 g; Carbs: 6 g; Protein: 1 g

Peanut "Pupsicles"

Preparation time: 15 minutes

Cooking time: 0 minutes

Servings: 10 (approximately 20-25 popsicles)

Ingredients:

- ¼ cup wheat germ
- ½ cup peanut butter
- 1 ripe banana
- ¼ cup chopped peanuts

Directions:

1. Combine the peanut butter, wheat germ, and mashed banana in a mixing bowl. Mix well.
2. Stir in the chopped peanuts.
3. Pour the mixture into popsicle molds or ice cube trays.
4. Freeze for at least 1 hour or until completely firm.
5. Remove from the molds or trays and serve.

Nutrition per serving: Calories: 144 kcal; Fat: 2 g; Carbs: 12 g; Protein: 22 g

Puppy's Tender Tummy Chicken Rice Meal

Preparation time: 5 minutes

Cooking time: 40 minutes

Servings: 6 cups

Ingredients:

- 1 cup white rice
- 4 cups water
- 2 boneless, skinless chicken breasts (about 1 lb)

Directions:

1. Bring 4 cups water to a boil over high heat in a large pot.
2. Add the chicken breasts to the pot and reduce the heat to low. Cover and simmer for 10-15 minutes until the chicken is cooked and no longer pink.
3. Remove the chicken from the pot and set it aside to cool.
4. Add the uncooked rice to the pot of chicken broth. Increase the heat to high and bring it to a boil.
5. Reduce the heat to low and cover the pot. Simmer for 20-25 minutes until the rice is tender and has absorbed most of the liquid.
6. While the rice is cooking, shred the cooked chicken into small pieces.
7. Add the shredded chicken to the pot once the rice is cooked. Stir to combine.
8. Allow the mixture to cool before serving your dog.
9. Store the leftovers in an airtight container in the refrigerator for up to 3 days, or freeze for up to 2 months.

Nutrition per serving: Calories: 150 kcal; Fat: 1.5 g; Carbs: 20 g; Protein: 16 g

Egg Spinach Sweet Potato Scramble

Preparation time: 5 minutes

Cooking time: 10 minutes

Servings: 2

Ingredients:

- 2 eggs
- ½ cup spinach, chopped
- 1 sweet potato, cubed
- 1 tbsp leek, chopped
- 1 pinch turmeric
- 1 tsp olive oil
- 1 pinch cumin
- 2 basil leaves, chopped

Directions:

1. Add the olive oil and heat over a medium fire in a skillet.
2. Beat the eggs in a bowl. Add turmeric and cumin to it. Mix.
3. Add the leek and sweet potato to the skillet.
4. Stir for 5 minutes. Add the eggs and stir for 1 minute.
5. Add the spinach and basil. Stir for 2 minutes. Serve.

Nutrition per serving: Calories: 220 kcal; Fat: 9 g; Carbs: 26 g; Protein: 11 g

Raw Breakfast

Preparation time: 5 minutes

Cooking time: 0 minutes

Servings: 1

Ingredients:

- 1 frozen raw veggie cupcake, thawed
- 1 tsp flaxseed oil
- ½ tsp raw honey
- 1 egg
- 2 tbsp plain yogurt or cottage cheese
- ½ tsp organic apple cider vinegar
- 1-ounce heart meat
- 1 chicken liver, rinsed

Directions:

1. Carefully crack your egg into a mixing bowl and grind the eggshell into fine small pieces.

2. Add the chicken liver with the heart meat, then stir in the honey, yogurt, flaxseed oil, and apple cider vinegar.
3. Serve it with a thawed Raw Veggie Cupcake for a full breakfast for your furry pal!

Nutrition per serving: Calories: 200 kcal; Fat: 10 g; Carbs: 10 g; Protein: 15 g

Doggy's Cheesy Breakfast

Preparation time: 5 minutes

Cooking time: 0 minutes

Servings: 1 cup

Ingredients:

- ⅓ cup mashed blueberries
- ⅓ cup plain yogurt
- ⅓ cup cottage cheese

Directions:

1. Mix all ingredients in a mixing bowl. Stir to combine.
2. If you have a small dog breed, you can serve them a portion and place the remainder of the mixture in the fridge for up to 5 days.

Nutrition per serving: Calories: 90 kcal; Fat: 1.5 g; Carbs: 9 g; Protein: 9 g

Hound's Fish Eggs

Preparation time: 8 minutes

Cooking time: 15 minutes

Servings: 2 cups

Ingredients:

- 4 eggs
- 1 can sardines in water
- 2 tbsp fresh parsley, finely chopped

Directions:

1. Begin by preheating your oven to 375°F. Coat a casserole dish with some nonstick cooking spray.
2. Drain the sardines; you can keep the water and use it to top your dog's food.
3. Chop the sardines and mix with the parsley.
4. Add the sardine mixture to the prepared casserole dish, then top with eggs. Crack the eggs over different portions of the sardine mixture, or you may beat them and then pour them over the mixture.
5. Bake for 15 minutes or until the eggs have cooked to the desired doneness.
6. Cool before serving it to your dog. You can keep it in the fridge for up to 3 days, or you may choose to freeze it in an airtight container.

Nutrition per serving: Calories: 256 kcal; Fat: 15 g; Carbs: 1 g; Protein: 26 g

Beetroot Yogurt Pudding

Preparation time: 2 hours

Cooking time: 5 minutes

Servings: 12

Ingredients:

- 2 cups beet cubes
- 2 cups Greek yogurt
- ½ tsp cinnamon
- 1 tbsp almond butter

Directions:

1. Boil the beets in water for 5 minutes.
2. Drain them, then add them to a blender.
3. Pour in the Greek yogurt. Add the almond butter and cinnamon.
4. Blend until smooth. Add to a silicon mold.

5. Freeze for 2 hours or until firm, then serve.

Nutrition per serving: Calories: 70 kcal; Fat: 1 g; Carbs: 9 g; Protein: 6 g

Molasses Pear Doggy Biscuits

Preparation time: 10 minutes

Cooking time: 30 minutes

Servings: 16 (3") biscuits

Ingredients:

- 2 ½ cups whole-wheat flour
- 2 cups pears, cored, seeds removed and chopped
- ¼ cup water
- 1 tbsp baking powder
- 3 tbsp molasses

Directions:

1. Preheat your oven to 350°F. Line a baking sheet with parchment paper.
2. Combine the ingredients in a large mixing bowl.
3. Turn your dough carefully onto a lightly floured surface and knead.
4. Roll out the dough to about ¼" thick, then slice it into 16 squares.
5. Bake your biscuits for 30 minutes or until the bottoms are golden brown.
6. Cook the biscuits entirely before serving them to your dog. Keep the biscuits in the fridge for up to 5 days, or place them in an airtight container and freeze them for up to 6 months.

Nutrition per serving: Calories: 92 kcal; Fat: 0.6 g; Carbs: 20.9 g; Protein: 2.1 g

Kelp and Alfalfa Powder Mix

Preparation time: 15 minutes

Cooking time: 0 minutes

Servings: Approximately 24 lb

Ingredients:

- 1 cup brewer's yeast
- 1 cup bone meal
- ½ cup kelp powder
- ½ cup alfalfa powder

Directions:

1. Mix well. Put the mixture in an air-tight container.
2. Place it in the freezer if desired.
3. Add one tablespoon to the dog's food every day.

Nutrition per serving: Calories: 21 kcal; Fat: 1 g; Carbs: 1 g; Protein: 12 g

Homemade Strawberry Shortcake

Preparation time: 30 minutes

Cooking time: 20 minutes

Servings: 1 cake

Ingredients:

- ½ cup plain yogurt
- 3 eggs
- 1 ½ cup wheat flour
- 1 tsp tapioca starch
- 3 tbsp honey
- 2 tbsp milk
- 3 tbsp coconut oil
- ¼ cup strawberries, choppedlentil spinach

Directions:

1. Add the flour to a bowl. Crack the eggs into it. Add the honey and oil. Mix well.
2. Pour the batter into a baking dish.
3. Place it in the oven, then bake for 15-20 minutes at 350°F.
4. Keep it aside to cool. Mix the yogurt, milk, and tapioca starch.

5. Pour the mixture on the cooled cake and top with strawberries. Serve.

Nutrition per serving: Calories: 977 kcal; Fat: 32 g; Carbs: 140 g; Protein: 32 g

Dehydrated Chicken Liver Treats

Preparation time: 15 minutes

Cooking time: 4 hours

Servings: 20-30 treats

Ingredients:

- 1 lb chicken liver, rinsed

Directions:

1. Using a nonstick spray, coat the dehydrator trays.
2. Flatten the livers slightly with a fork if they are too thick.
3. Arrange the livers on the dehydrator trays neatly, leaving space between them so the edges can dry properly.
4. Dehydrate the livers for about 4 hours, swapping the drying tray's position halfway through.
5. Allow to cool completely and store in the refrigerator for 3 to 4 days or in a sealed container in the freezer for up to 6 months.
6. Note: Dehydrating time may vary depending on the dehydrator.

Nutrition per serving: Calories: 15 kcal; Fat: 0.5 g; Carbs: 0.5 g; Protein: 2.5 g

Puppy Mango Sorbet

Preparation time: 5 minutes

Cooking time: 0 minutes

Servings: 2 cups

Ingredients:

- juice from 1 lime
- juice from 1 orange
- ½ cup unsweetened almond milk
- 2 ripe mangoes, peeled and seed removed

Directions:

1. Place all ingredients in a blender and purée them.
2. Transfer the mixture to an ice cube tray.
3. Place in the freezer overnight.
4. Once the treats are frozen, transfer them into a zip-lock freezer bag to store for up to 2 months in your freezer.

Nutrition per serving: Calories: 110 kcal; Fat: 1 g; Carbs: 27 g; Protein: 2 g

Homemade Vegetables and Turkey

Preparation time: 30 minutes

Cooking time: 0 minutes

Servings: 1 bowl

Ingredients:

- 1 cup turkey breast, minced
- 1 cup cooked rice
- 1 can mixed vegetables, drained

Directions:

1. Place the turkey in a chopper and mince.
2. Add the rice and mixed vegetables. Combine well.
3. Store in refrigerator for up to 2 days. Serve.

Nutrition per serving: Calories: 450 kcal; Fat: 3 g; Carbs: 75 g; Protein: 34 g

Eggshell Calcium

Preparation time: 5 minutes

Cooking time: 15 minutes

Servings: About 12 tsp

Ingredients:

- 12 eggshells

Directions:

1. Wash the eggshells and place them in the refrigerator to dry.
2. Preheat your oven to 200°F.
3. Arrange the eggshells neatly on a cookie sheet and bake for 10-15 minutes or more. The eggshells need to be completely dry before grinding.
4. Place the dried eggshells in a clean blender and grind until it is extremely smooth (you can also do this using a mortar and pestle).
5. Pour the ground eggshells into a jar with a lid and seal it tightly. Store in a dry place for a maximum of 2 months.

Nutrition per serving: Calories: 20 kcal; Fat: 0 g; Carbs: 1 g; Protein: 1 g

Yogurt and Watermelon Frozen Treats

Preparation time: 15 minutes

Cooking time: 0 minutes

Servings: Approximately 23 lb

Ingredients:

- 2 cups seedless watermelon, diced
- 1 cup plain yogurt

Directions:

1. Blend the watermelon in a blender or food processor until smooth.
2. Place about one tablespoon of yogurt into each opening of the mold.
3. Fill the remaining space of the mold with the pureed watermelon.
4. Place the treats in the freezer and let them freeze for 4 hours.

5. Once frozen, remove the treats from the mold, then store them in a freezer bag or airtight container.

Nutrition per serving: Calories: 13 kcal; Fat: 0.1 g; Carbs: 2.4 g; Protein: 0.8 g

Pup's Liver Quiché

Preparation time: 10 minutes

Cooking time: 30 minutes

Servings: 6 puppy muffins

Ingredients:

- 3 eggs
- ¼ lb chicken livers, rinsed and cooked
- ¼ cup cooked green beans

Directions:

1. Begin by preheating your oven to 350°F—grease the muffin tins.
2. Mash the chicken livers and chop them into small bits.
3. In a mixing bowl, whisk your eggs. Add the green beans and chicken livers with the eggs.
4. Fill the muffin tins ¾ full of mixture, then bake the muffins for 30 minutes or until golden brown.
5. Let the muffins cool completely before serving them to your special puppy pal!

Nutrition per serving: Calories: 85 kcal; Fat: 4 g; Carbs: 2 g; Protein: 8 g

Fruity Chicken

Preparation time: 15 minutes

Cooking time: 0 minutes

Servings: 6

Ingredients:

- ¾ cup celery, sliced

- 1 tbsp pineapple juice
- 2 cups chicken, cooked and cut into cubes
- ¾ cup fresh peaches, peeled and cubed
- 1 tbsp apple cider vinegar
- ¾ cup melon, cubed
- ½ cup plain yogurt or sour cream

Directions:

1. Add the chicken to a bowl. Add the peaches, celery, and melon. Toss gently.
2. Mix the yogurt or sour cream, apple cider vinegar, and pineapple juice separately. Pour them over the salad.
3. Combine gently and serve immediately. Spoon your dog's portion over his usual food and serve.

Nutrition per serving: Calories: 261 kcal; Fat: 9 g; Carbs: 15 g; Protein: 29 g

Turkey Oatmeal Doggy Biscuits

Preparation time: 10 minutes

Cooking time: 25 minutes

Servings: 24 (2") biscuits

Ingredients:

- 1 ¾ cup whole-wheat flour
- 1 ½ cup shredded turkey or chicken
- 1 tsp baking powder
- 2 ½ cups quick-cooking oats
- 1 cup turkey or chicken broth

Directions:

1. Preheat your oven to 350°F—line two baking sheets with parchment paper.
2. Combine the biscuit's dry ingredients in a bowl and set aside.
3. Add the turkey and broth to your blender, and blend until you have the consistency of baby food.
4. Add this meat mixture to your dry ingredients and mix well.

5. Turn your dough out on a lightly floured surface and knead.
6. It will be a heavy dough, so it will take some effort to roll it out and cut it into shapes. Place the cut shapes onto prepared baking sheets.
7. Bake the biscuits for 25 minutes or until they are golden brown.
8. Make sure to cool the biscuits before serving your dog.
9. Keep the biscuits in your fridge for up to 3 days, or place them in an airtight container and freeze for up to 6 months.

Nutrition per serving: Calories: 70 kcal; Fat: 1.5 g; Carbs: 10 g; Protein: 4 g

Fruit & Yogurt Treat

Preparation time: 1 hour

Cooking time: 0 minutes

Servings: 6

Ingredients:

- 1 cup unsweetened yogurt
- ⅓ cup chopped strawberries
- ¼ cup blueberries
- 1 pinch cinnamon

Directions:

1. In a bowl, combine the yogurt with cinnamon.
2. Add the fruits to it.
3. Add the mixture to a silicon mold. Freeze them for 1 hour.
4. Ready to serve.

Nutrition per serving: Calories: 80 kcal; Fat: 0.5 g; Carbs: 13 g; Protein: 7 g

Banana, Vanilla Yogurt Dip

Preparation time: 20 minutes

Cooking time: 0minutes

Servings: Approximately 29 lb

Ingredients:

- 3 tbsp peanut butter
- 2 tbsp honey
- 1 banana
- 16 oz vanilla yogurt
- 1 tbsp whole wheat flour

Directions:

1. Mix the fruit, honey, and peanut butter until well blended.
2. In a separate bowl, combine the yogurt and flour. Mix well.
3. Add the fruit mixture to the yogurt and blend. Refrigerate.
4. Use this dip to coat biscuits and treats.
5. Refrigerate until the coating is set and firm.

Nutrition per serving: Calories: 31 kcal; Fat: 2 g; Carbs: 4 g; Protein: 5 g

Tuna Casserole

Preparation time: 10 minutes

Cooking time: 0 minutes

Servings: 2 cups

Ingredients:

- ¼ cup grated parmesan cheese
- 1 cup cooked pasta, drained
- 1 (9-ounce) can tuna packed in water
- ¼ cup chopped fresh parsley
- ½ cup frozen peas, thawed

Directions:

1. Drain the canned tuna and discard the liquid or reserve it again.
2. Add tuna, peas, pasta, cheese, and parsley into a mixing bowl. Mix well and serve.
3. Store the leftovers in the refrigerator for up to 3 days or keep them in a sealed container, then store them in the freezer for up to 3 months.

Nutrition per serving: Calories: 315 kcal; Fat: 7 g; Carbs: 27 g; Protein: 34 g

Homemade Applesauce Dog Treats

Preparation time: 20 minutes

Cooking time: 25 minutes

Servings: 4 servings

Ingredients:

- ¾ cup unsweetened applesauce
- 3 ¼ cups wheat flour
- 1 egg
- ½ cup water
- 1 tsp cinnamon

Directions:

1. Add all the ingredients into a bowl, then mix well.
2. Pour into molds—place them in the oven. Bake for 20-25 minutes at 350°F.
3. Allow to cool completely and serve.

Nutrition per serving: Calories: 397 kcal; Fat: 2.7 g; Carbs: 87.3 g; Protein: 12.5 g

Yummy Homemade Meat Cakes

Preparation time: 30 minutes

Cooking time: 40-45 minutes

Servings: 36 cakes

Ingredients:

- ¼ cup olive oil
- 3 cups water
- 1 ½ cup brown rice
- 4 grated carrots
- 1 ½ cup rolled oats
- 2 potatoes, grated
- ¼ tsp salt
- 2 celery stalks, chopped
- 8 eggs
- 6 lb ground beef

Directions:

1. Cook rice, let it cool, and fluff.
2. Add carrots, eggs, ground beef, potatoes, celery, oats, salt, and olive oil. Combine well.
3. Form balls with the mixture and place them in muffin tins.
4. Place the muffin tins in the oven, then bake for 40-45 minutes at 400°F.
5. Allow cooling before serving.

Nutrition per serving: Calories: 185 kcal; Fat: 9.5 g; Carbs: 9.8 g; Protein: 14.2 g

Applesauce Peanut Butter Doggy Biscuits

Preparation time: 10 minutes

Cooking time: 25 minutes

Servings: 36 (2") biscuits

Ingredients:

- 2 cups oats
- 3 cups whole-wheat flour
- 1 tsp baking powder
- 1 cup unsweetened applesauce
- 1 cup organic peanut butter

Directions:

1. Preheat your oven to 350°F. Place two baking sheets with parchment paper.

2. Mix all the doggy biscuit ingredients in a large mixing bowl, stirring until well combined.
3. Knead your doggy dough on a lightly floured surface. If the mixture is too crumbly, you may have to add a teaspoon of olive oil.
4. Roll your dough out so it is about ¼" thick. Cut your dough into 36 desired shapes and place them onto prepared baking sheets.
5. Bake the doggy biscuits for 25 minutes or until lightly browned.
6. Remove the biscuits from the oven, then allow completely cooling before serving to your pooch.
7. Keep the doggy biscuits in your fridge for up to 5 days, or place them in an airtight container and freeze the treats for up to 6 months.

Nutrition per serving: Calories: 60 kcal; Fat: 2 g; Carbs: 8 g; Protein: 2 g

Crockpot Beef and Rice Dog Food

Preparation time: 30 minutes

Cooking time: 5 hours

Servings: About 4 cups

Ingredients:

- 2 ½ lb ground beef
- 4 cups water
- 1 can kidney beans drained
- 1 ½ cup brown rice
- 1 ½ cup chopped squash
- ½ cup peas
- 1 ½ cup chopped carrots

Directions:

1. Add all ingredients to a crockpot. Mix well.
2. Set the crockpot to low heat. Cook on Low for 5 hours.

3. Allow to cool, and serve.
4. Store the leftovers in the refrigerator for a maximum of 5 days.

Nutrition per serving: Calories: 638 kcal; Fat: 36 g; Carbs: 36 g; Protein: 40 g

Homemade Doggy Meatballs

Preparation time: 30 minutes

Cooking time: 25-30 minutes

Servings: 20 meatballs

Ingredients:

- ½ cup diced carrots
- 1 egg
- 1 lb lean ground beef
- ⅔ cup breadcrumbs
- ½ cup shredded cheddar cheese

Directions:

1. Add all ingredients into a bowl, then mix well until everything sticks together.
2. Make meatballs out of the mixture. Arrange them onto a sheet pan.
3. Bake in the oven for 25-30 minutes at 350°F.
4. Let it cool down before you serve it, or put it in the fridge.

Nutrition per serving: Calories: 61 kcal; Fat: 3.5 g; Carbs: 2.6 g; Protein: 4.2 g

Homemade Recipes for Junior Dog

Quick Mushroom and Veggie

Preparation time: 5 minutes

Cooking time: 8 minutes

Servings: 2

Ingredients:

- 1 carrot, sliced
- ½ cup mushroom, cut into wedges
- ½ cup green beans
- ⅓ tsp cinnamon
- 1 basil powder pinch
- 1 cup water

Directions:

1. Add the carrots, green beans, mushroom, and one cup of water to a pot.
2. Bring it to a boil.
3. Add the cinnamon and basil powder.
4. Cook until the water evaporates. Serve.

Nutrition per serving: Calories: 40 kcal; Fat: 0.5 g; Carbs: 8 g; Protein: 2 g

Banana Biscuits

Preparation time: 30 minutes

Cooking time: 12 minutes

Servings: 20

Ingredients:

- 2 cups whole flour
- ½ cup banana puree
- ½ cup almond butter
- 1 tsp cinnamon
- 2 eggs

Directions:

1. Add wax paper to a cookie sheet.
2. Beat the eggs in a mixing bowl.
3. Add the almond butter and banana puree.
4. Beat well. Fold in the cinnamon and whole flour.
5. Knead well and let it rest for some time.
6. Roll it out, and then cut it into any shape.
7. Arrange them on the cookie sheet.
8. Bake for 12 minutes. Serve at room temperature.

Nutrition per serving: Calories: 110 kcal; Fat: 6 g; Carbs: 11 g; Protein: 4 g

Lentil Spinach Rice Dish

Preparation time: 5 minutes

Cooking time: 20 minutes

Servings: 4

Ingredients:

- ½ cup rice
- ⅓ cup lentils
- ¼ cup sweet potato cubes
- ½ cup chicken slices
- 1 cup chicken broth
- ½ tsp cinnamon
- ½ tsp basil powder
- 1 cup spinach leaves

Directions:

1. Add the rice, lentil, and chicken slices to a pot.
2. Add the sweet potatoes.
3. Then, add cinnamon and basil powder and spinach leaves.

4. Pour in the chicken broth.
5. Stir once and cover with a lid. Cook for 20 minutes. Serve.

Nutrition per serving: Calories: 250 kcal; Fat: 2 g; Carbs: 45 g; Protein: 15 g

Non-Fat Yogurt Pups

Preparation time: 20 minutes

Cooking time: 0 minutes

Servings: Approximately 22 lb

Ingredients:

- 16 oz plain non-fat yogurt
- 1 tbsp chicken bouillon granules
- ⅔ cup water

Directions:

1. Dissolve bouillon in water.
2. Add yogurt and blend thoroughly.
3. Pour the mixture into small containers.
4. Refrigerate.

Nutrition per serving: Calories: 11 kcal; Fat: 0 g; Carbs: 1 g; Protein: 2 g

Homemade Peanut Butter Dog Treats

Preparation time: 15 minutes

Cooking time: 0 minutes

Servings: 20 balls

Ingredients:

- 3 cups old fashion oats
- ¼ cup milk
- ¼ cup peanut butter
- 1 cup pumpkin puree

Directions:

1. Add 2 ½ cups of oats to a bowl. Add peanut butter, pumpkin, and milk. Combine well.
2. Form balls out of the mixture.
3. Roll the balls in the remaining ½ cup of oats.
4. Keep the mixture in the refrigerator until the balls are firm enough.
5. Store for up to a week.

Nutrition per serving: Calories: 90 kcal; Fat: 2.8 g; Carbs: 14 g; Protein: 3 g

One-Pot Rice and Veggie Dish

Preparation time: 5 minutes

Cooking time: 20 minutes

Servings: 4

Ingredients:

- ½ cup rice
- ¼ cup peas
- ¼ cup carrot, sliced
- ½ cup boiled kidney beans
- ½ tsp cinnamon
- ½ tsp basil powder
- 1 cup chicken broth
- 1 tsp olive oil

Directions:

1. Place the rice, kidney beans, carrots, and peas in a deep dish.
2. Add the olive oil on top.
3. Add the cinnamon and basil powder.
4. Pour in the chicken broth. Cover with a lid.
5. Cook for 20 minutes on medium heat. Serve.

Nutrition per serving: Calories: 180 kcal; Fat: 1.5 g; Carbs: 34 g; Protein: 7 g

Mixed Blueberry and Strawberry Parfait for Dogs

Preparation time: 15 minutes

Cooking time: 0 minutes

Servings: Approximately 24 lb

Ingredients:

- 1 cup plain, nonfat yogurt
- 1 cup blueberries, chopped
- 1 cup strawberries, chopped
- 1 cup applesauce, unsweetened

Directions:

1. Add yogurt, blueberries, strawberries, and applesauce into a blender and blend until smooth.
2. Transfer the mixture to an airtight container. Refrigerate until use. It can last for 7 days.
3. Remove ¼ cupof the parfait and serve. Refrigerate the remaining.

Nutrition per serving: Calories: 20 kcal; Fat: 0.2 g; Carbs: 4 g; Protein: 1 g

Kidney Bean Green Bean Brown Rice

Preparation time: 5 minutes

Cooking time: 15 minutes

Servings: 2

Ingredients:

- ½ cup brown rice
- ¼ cup green beans, diced
- 1 carrot, cubed
- 1 sweet potato, cubed
- ¼ cup boiled kidney beans
- 1 pinch turmeric
- ½ tsp olive oil
- 1 pinch cinnamon

- 1 pinch basil powder
- 1 cup water

Directions:

1. In a pot, add the olive oil. Toss the kidney beans for 1 minute.
2. Add the brown rice, sweet potatoes, and spices.
3. Stir for 1 minute and pour in 1 cup water.
4. Bring it to a boil. Add the carrot and green beans.
5. Cook until the water evaporates. Serve.

Nutrition per serving: Calories: 320 kcal; Fat: 2 g; Carbs: 68 g; Protein: 9 g

Wallace's Spinach Sprats

Preparation time: 5 minutes

Cooking time: 5 minutes

Servings: 6 cups

Ingredients:

- 2 tbsp olive oil
- 3 large eggs
- 2 cups spinach, chopped
- 2 cups cooked brown rice, chilled
- 1 (8.5-ounce) sprat can, drained and chopped

Directions:

1. Spray a large skillet with some nonstick cooking spray.
2. In a small bowl, whip the eggs with a fork. Pour the eggs into the prepared skillet over medium-high heat. Cook for a few minutes or until the eggs are firm, then remove from heat.
3. Remove the eggs from the skillet and slice them into strips.
4. Place the skillet back over heat and add in the olive oil. Add the rice and stir often until warmed, then add the spinach.

Cook until your spinach wilts, then add the sprats and eggs and mix.

5. Cool the mixture before serving. Keep it in your fridge for up to 3 days, or place it in an airtight container and freeze for up to 6 months.

Nutrition per serving: Calories: 300 kcal; Fat: 15 g; Carbs: 25 g; Protein: 15 g

Baked Chicken Satay

Preparation time: 5 minutes

Cooking time: 20 minutes

Servings: 10

Ingredients:

- 2 chicken breasts
- ½ tsp cinnamon
- ½ tsp turmeric
- ¼ tsp cumin
- ⅓ tsp olive oil

Directions:

1. Add aluminum foil to a baking tray.
2. Place a grilling wire rack on top.
3. Cut the chicken into thin strips.
4. Coat them in olive oil, cumin, turmeric, and cinnamon.
5. Place them on a stand.
6. Bake for 10 minutes and flip them.
7. Bake for another 10 minutes. Rest for 5 minutes. Serve.

Nutrition per serving: Calories: 120 kcal; Fat: 2 g; Carbs: 1 g; Protein: 24 g

Raw Dog Treats

Preparation time: 15 minutes

Cooking time: 0 minutes

Servings: 30 treats

Ingredients:

- 1 egg
- 1 lb ground sirloin
- 1 cup finely chopped raw pumpkin seeds
- 2 tbsp molasses

Directions:

1. Using parchment paper, line a cookie sheet.
2. Crack the egg into a large bowl. Add in sirloin and molasses. Mix well.
3. On a separate parchment paper, pour out chopped raw pumpkin seeds.
4. Pinch off small amounts of the meat mixture, then shape them into balls about 1 inch in size. Then, roll the meatballs in chopped pumpkin seeds.
5. Arrange the balls neatly on the cookie sheet and freeze them overnight.
6. Once frozen, retrieve the balls from the freezer and remove them from the cookie sheet, then store them in plastic bags with zip tops. Store them in the freezer for a maximum of 6 months.

Nutrition per serving: Calories: 40 kcal; Fat: 2 g; Carbs: 1 g; Protein: 3 g

Terrier Chicken Meatloaf

Preparation time: 10 minutes

Cooking time: 1 hour and 45 minutes

Servings: 8 cups

Ingredients:

- 4 cups chicken broth
- ½ cup barley
- 1 tbsp olive oil
- ½ lb ground chicken
- ½ cup rolled oats
- ¾ cup carrots, finely chopped
- 2 whole eggs
- ½ cup low-fat cottage cheese

- 1 ½ lb ground chicken

Directions:

1. In a saucepan, bring your barley and chicken broth to a boil, and reduce to a simmer for 45 minutes. Set aside to cool.
2. Preheat your oven to 350°F. Grease lightly a baking dish with nonstick cooking spray.
3. Mix the ground chicken, rolled oats, carrots, cottage cheese, eggs, and olive oil in a huge mixing bowl. Mix well.
4. Slowly add the cooled broth and barley to the mixture.
5. Add to the prepared baking dish and bake for 1 hour.
6. Cool before serving to your pooch. Place it in the fridge for up to 3 days in an airtight container, and freeze for 6 months.

Nutrition per serving: Calories: 280 kcal; Fat: 10 g; Carbs: 15 g; Protein: 25 g

Almond Banana Dog Treat

Preparation time: 1 hour

Cooking time: 10 minutes

Servings: 2

Ingredients:

- 1 ½ cup Greek yogurt
- 2 tbsp almond butter
- 1 banana, cut into slices

Directions:

1. Melt the almond butter.
2. Mash the banana perfectly.
3. Combine the banana with the almond butter.
4. Add the Greek yogurt.
5. Mix well. Add the mixture to a silicon mold.

6. Freeze for 1 hour or longer. They are ready to serve.

Nutrition per serving: Calories: 195 kcal; Fat: 8 g; Carbs: 17 g; Protein: 14 g

Frozen Banana and Peanut Treats

Preparation time: 20 minutes

Cooking time: 0 minutes

Servings: Approximately 16 lb

Ingredients:

- 4 cups plain yogurt
- 3 medium ripe bananas (peeled and mashed)
- 2 tbsp smooth peanut butter

Directions:

1. Using a food blender, blitz all ingredients until pureed.
2. Pour the mixture into popsicle trays or ice cube trays. Freeze for 2-3 hours or until completely solid.

Nutrition per serving: Calories: 32 kcal; Fat: 0.5 g; Carbs: 4.5 g; Protein: 2.5 g

Homemade Dry Dog Food

Preparation time: 30 minutes

Cooking time: 40-45 minutes

Servings: 2 cups

Ingredients:

- ½ cup brown rice
- 2 cups oatmeal
- 6 oz plain yogurt
- 1 lb ground venison
- 2 tbsp corn oil
- Apple, small, ground
- 1 cup ground green beans

Directions:

1. Mix the yogurt, venison, oats, green beans, corn oil, apple, and rice in a bowl.
2. Mix well, then spread out on a sheet pan.
3. Bake for 40-45 minutes or until firm, at 350°F.
4. Allow it to cool, and cut it into small bite-size pieces.
5. Keep it in an airtight container for a maximum of one week.

Nutrition per serving: Calories: 760 kcal; Fat: 24 g; Carbs: 84 g; Protein: 53 g

Spinach Omelet

Preparation time: 10 minutes

Cooking time: 10 minutes

Servings: 1 omelet

Ingredients:

- 1 cup baby spinach leaves, torn
- 2 eggs
- 1 tbsp grated parmesan cheese

Directions:

1. Crack the eggs into your small bowl, then whisk. Add the cheese and spinach. Grease a nonstick skillet with cooking spray, then pour the egg mixture into it.
2. Cook over medium heat until partially done. Using a spatula, flip the omelet and then allow it to cook to the desired doneness.
3. Allow to cool before serving or storing. Keep any remaining food in the fridge for a maximum of three days.

Nutrition per serving: Calories: 240 kcal; Fat: 16 g; Carbs: 3 g; Protein: 20 g

Giblet Gravy

Preparation time: 10 minutes

Cooking time: 60 minutes

Servings: About 4 cups

Ingredients:

- 2 cups chicken broth
- Neck and giblets from 1 turkey
- 1 tbsp vegetable oil
- 2–3 tbsp all-purpose flour
- 1 carrot, chopped
- 1 celery rib, chopped
- 4 cups water

Directions:

1. Heat vegetable oil in a saucepan over a medium-high fire. Add the turkey neck and giblets. Brown the turkey and add the remaining ingredients except for the all-purpose flour.
2. Simmer for 50-60 minutes. Take off from the heat.
3. Strain the broth and skim off the fat. Discard fat.
4. Remove the bones from the meat, discard them, then dice the boneless meat.
5. Add turkey meat to broth. Add the all-purpose flour and stir while reheating. Bring the mixture to a boil, stirring regularly, 'til it thickens.
6. Transfer from heat to a bowl and let it cool. Serve. Keep it in the refrigerator for up to 3 days or store it in a sealed container in the freezer for up to 6 months.

Nutrition per serving: Calories: 50 kcal; Fat: 3 g; Carbs: 2 g; Protein: 4 g

Frozen Strawberry and Banana Smoothie Treat

Preparation time: 15 minutes

Cooking time: 0 minutes

Servings: Approximately 22 lb

Ingredients:

- 2 bags frozen strawberries (16 oz each)
- 2 bananas, sliced
- 6 tbsp honey
- 3 cups plain, low-fat Greek yogurt
- ½ cup skim milk

Directions:

1. Add strawberries, yogurt, banana, honey, yogurt, and skim milk into a blender, then blend until smooth.
2. Pour into molds and freeze until firm.
3. Remove from the molds and serve.
4. Transfer the remaining treats into Ziploc bags and freeze.

Nutrition per serving: Calories: 88 kcal; Fat: 0.5 g; Carbs: 18 g; Protein: 5 g

Chicken and Greens for Beginners

Preparation time: 30 minutes

Cooking time: 0 minutes

Servings: Approximately 27-28 lb

Ingredients:

- 11 lb chicken thighs, breasts, chopped into pieces
- 3.3 lb ground chicken bones
- 6.6 lb chicken hearts and liver
- 2.2 lb celery, finely chopped
- 1.1 lb broccoli, finely chopped
- 2.2 lb carrots, finely chopped
- 2.2 lb spinach, finely chopped
- 3 chicken eggs, lightly boiled

Directions:

1. Add chicken thighs or breasts, ground chicken bones, organ meat, eggs (with their shells), carrots, celery, spinach, and broccoli into a mixing bowl. Mix until well combined.

2. Make portions and place them in separate bags or lunch boxes. Keep 1 bag in the refrigerator to use and the rest of the bags in the freezer.
3. Use within 2-3 weeks. Remove one bag from the freezer daily and place it in the refrigerator to thaw.
4. Serve at room temperature or warm.

Nutrition per serving: Calories: 335 kcal; Fat: 18 g; Carbs: 9 g; Protein: 32 g

Strawberry and Kiwi Yogurt Treats

Preparation time: 10 minutes

Cooking time: 0 minutes

Servings: Approximately 24 lb

Ingredients:

- 8 oz strawberry yogurt
- 2 kiwi fruit, mashed

Directions:

1. Mix, and freeze in an ice cube tray.
2. Serve.

Nutrition per serving: Calories: 10 kcal; Fat: 0.1 g; Carbs: 1.9 g; Protein: 0.6 g

Mutt Meatloaf Meal

Preparation time: 15 minutes

Cooking time: 50-60 minutes

Servings: 16 cups

Ingredients:

- 2 cups puréed green beans, steamed
- ½ lb organic beef liver or chicken liver, rinsed and diced
- 2 cups puréed potatoes, steamed
- 4 lb lean ground turkey
- 2 cups puréed carrots, steamed
- 4 eggs

Directions:

1. Turn the temperature in the oven up to 350°F.
2. Mix all of the ingredients, then spread them among four loaf pans. Each should be around three-quarters filled. Bake for 50-60 minutes. Drain out any grease.
3. Freeze any leftover meatloaf by placing it in a plastic bag with a zip-top closure and keeping it in the freezer for up to six months.

Nutrition per serving: Calories: 250 kcal; Fat: 10 g; Carbs: 10 g; Protein: 25 g

Vegan Homemade Dog Food

Preparation time: 30 minutes

Cooking time: 60 minutes

Servings: 2 cups

Ingredients:

- 1 banana, sliced
- 1 package frozen pea
- 1 sweet potato, chopped
- 1 ⅓ cup water
- ⅔ cup quinoa

Directions:

1. Put water into a pot and add quinoa. Cook the quinoa till it is done, then drain the liquid.
2. Place it in the oven and bake for 50-60 minutes at 350°F.
3. Mix the quinoa, sweet potato, peas, and banana in a bowl.
4. Serve. Keep the leftovers in the refrigerator for 3 days or store them in an airtight container in the freezer for up to 6 months.

Nutrition per serving: Calories: 320 kcal; Fat: 1.6 g; Carbs: 64 g; Protein: 10 g

Doggy's Salmon Balls

Preparation time: 5 minutes

Cooking time: 15 minutes

Servings: 12 (2") balls

Ingredients:

- 1 egg
- 1 tbsp olive oil
- 1 cup cooked brown rice
- 1 ½ cup cooked salmon, chopped

Directions:

1. Preheat your oven to 350°F. Lightly grease a baking sheet.
2. In your mixing bowl, combine all of your ingredients. Use a melon baller or spoon to roll the mixture into 12 balls—place the balls on the prepared baking sheet.
3. Bake the salmon balls for 15 minutes. Allow your doggy salmon balls to cool before serving. Keep the salmon balls in your fridge for up to 3 days, or freeze them in an airtight container for up to 6 months.

Nutrition per serving: Calories: 120 kcal; Fat: 4.5 g; Carbs: 10 g; Protein: 8 g

Canine Slow-Cooked Chicken Meal

Preparation time: 10 minutes

Cooking time: 12 hours

Servings: 9 cups

Ingredients:

- 3 chicken breasts, boneless and skinless
- 1 cup uncooked brown rice
- ½ cup cranberries
- 1 sweet potato, peeled and cubed
- 2 large carrots, sliced into 1"-inch rounds
- water as needed

Directions:

1. Add all your ingredients to your slow cooker and cover with water.
2. Cook on low setting overnight, for about 12 hours.
3. Cool the mixture before serving your dog. Keep the mixture in your fridge for up to 3 days, place it in an airtight container, and freeze for up to 6 months.

Nutrition per serving: Calories: 250 kcal; Fat: 5 g; Carbs: 30 g; Protein: 20 g

Blueberry "Pupsicles"

Preparation time: 25minutes

Cooking time: 0 minutes

Servings: Approximately 20 lb

Ingredients:

- 16 oz plain yogurt, non-fat
- 1 cup blueberries, washed and dried

Directions:

1. Place the yogurt and the blueberries into a blender and blend. Divide the mixture between 4 to 8 miniature Dixie cups. You can freeze them as is or insert a stick in the middle for supervised consumption.
2. Place the Dixie cup in the freezer and freeze for at least 4 hours. Store the unused popsicles in the freezer until ready to feed to your dog.

Nutrition per serving: Calories: 25 kcal; Fat: 0.2 g; Carbs: 3.8 g; Protein: 2.4 g

Raw Meat and Yoghurt for Dinner

Preparation time: 15 minutes

Cooking time: 0 minutes

Servings: Approximately 12 lb

Ingredients:

- ¾ oz raw meat
- 1 egg raw
- 2 tbsp yogurt
- 1 tsp honey
- 1 tbsp apple cider vinegar
- ½ tsp flax seed oil
- 1 tsp kelp seaweed powder
- 1 tsp alfalfa powder
- 1 tsp vitamin C for dogs
- ¼ cup kibble optional

Directions:

1. Mix all ingredients and serve.
2. Refrigerate if served later. Unfinished portions should be disposed of to avoid bacterial infection.

Nutrition per serving: Calories: 85 kcal; Fat: 1 g; Carbs: 2 g; Protein: 9 g

Fruits and Vegetable Breakfast

Preparation time: 15 minutes

Cooking time: 0 minutes

Servings: Approximately 2 1 lb

Ingredients:

- ⅓ cup vegetables
- ⅓ cup rolled oats
- ½ cup yogurt
- 1 tsp vitamin C for dogs, crushed
- 1 tsp honey
- 1 tsp apple cider vinegar
- 1 tsp kelp seaweed powder, shredded and lightly steamed.
- Fruits/vegetables, apples, 1 stalk of celery, ½ cup broccoli florets, a handful of spinach, 1 large carrot, etc.
- 1 tsp alfalfa powder
- 1 tsp flax seed oil

Directions:

1. Soak the rolled oats in yogurt overnight.
2. Mix all ingredients and serve.

Nutrition per serving: Calories: 23 kcal; Fat: 1 g; Carbs: 0.5 g; Protein: 8 g

Salmon and Vegetables Meatballs

Preparation time: 25 minutes

Cooking time: 0 minutes

Servings: Approximately (50-100 lb)

Ingredients:

- 4 lb frozen fish fillets like mackerel or whiting
- ½ -1lb beef liver
- 2 cans Alaskan wild pink salmon
- 2-6 eggs (optional)
- 1 large carrot, cut into small pieces (about 1 cup), cooked
- 1 cup broccoli, cut into small florets, cooked
- 1 cup yam, cut into small pieces, cooked
- 1 large apple, cored, cut into small pieces
- 1 cup raw pumpkin seeds (pepitas)
- 4 tbsp dried oregano
- 4 tbsp dried parsley
- 4 tbsp honey
- 4 tbspThorvinkelp powder
- 4 tbsp turmeric powder
- 2 cups cooked oatmeal or barley or brown rice (optional)

Directions:

1. Using a meat grinder, grind the frozen fish, liver, carrots, broccoli, yam, apple, and pepitas into a large bowl.
2. Add salmon, eggs, oregano, parsley, honey, oatmeal if using, and kelp powder. Mix well.
3. Make meatballs and place them on a baking sheet. Freeze until firm.
4. Make portions and place them in separate bags or lunch boxes. Keep 1 bag

in the refrigerator to use and the rest of the bags in the freezer.

5. Use within 2-3 weeks. Remove one bag from the freezer daily and place it in the refrigerator to thaw.
6. Serve at room temperature or warm.

Nutrition per serving: Calories: 169 kcal; Fat: 6 g; Carbs: 8 g; Protein: 18 g

Spinach and Chicken Muffins for Dogs

Preparation time: 5 minutes

Cooking time: 15 minutes

Servings: 6

Ingredients:

- 2 eggs
- 1 cup almond flour
- ½ cup cooked, shredded chicken breast
- ½ cup spinach, chopped
- ¼ cup unsweetened applesauce
- ¼ cup low-fat, unsalted cottage cheese
- ¼ tsp baking powder

Directions:

1. Preheat the oven to 350°F and grease a muffin tin with oil or cooking spray.
2. In a mixing bowl, whisk the eggs until lightly beaten.
3. Add the almond flour, baking powder, and unsweetened applesauce. Mix well.
4. Add the shredded chicken breast, chopped spinach, and low-fat cottage cheese. Mix until well combined.
5. Spoon the batter into the muffin tin, filling each cup about 3/4 full.
6. Bake for 20-25 minutes, or until a toothpick inserted into the center of a muffin comes out clean.
7. Allow the muffins to cool before serving.

Nutrition per serving: Calories: 170 kcal; Fat: 10 g; Carbs: 7 g; Protein: 13 g

Beef and Rice

Preparation time: 10 minutes

Cooking time: 10 minutes

Servings:

Ingredients:

- 2 cups brown rice, cooked
- ¼ pound ground beef
- 3 pieces wheat bread
- 1 hard-boiled egg
- 1 tsp calcium carbonate powder

Directions:

1. Heat a pan and add the ground beef. Brown it and cook it thoroughly.
2. Remove the shell from the egg, then chop the egg into small bits.
3. Chop the bread into bite-size pieces.
4. Place the cooked ground beef into a bowl. Add the remaining ingredients and combine. Mix well.
5. Serve.

Nutrition per serving: Calories: 450 kcal; Fat: 10 g; Carbs: 50 g; Protein: 20 g

Zoe's Buffalo Meatballs

Preparation time: 10 minutes

Cooking time: 10 minutes

Servings: 30 (1") meatballs

Ingredients:

- ½ cup milk
- 1 lb ground bison
- 1 egg

- 2 slices whole-wheat bread, sliced into ½" cubes
- ⅓ cup parmesan cheese, grated
- 2 tbsp parsley, chopped
- olive oil for frying

Directions:

1. Soak your bread cubes in the milk in a mixing bowl for about 5 minutes. Remove the bread from the milk, then squeeze out excess milk and discard it.
2. Combine your egg, cheese, bread cubes, bison, and parsley in a mixing bowl. Take out small pieces and roll them into meatballs.
3. In a skillet, heat ½ cup of olive oil over a medium-high fire. Fry each meatball until they are no longer pink in the center, for about 10 minutes.
4. Remove the meatballs from the heat and allow them to cool before serving your canine pal. Keep in the fridge for 3-4 days or place it in an airtight container, then freeze for up to 6 months.

Nutrition per serving: Calories: 80 kcal; Fat: 4 g; Carbs: 3 g; Protein: 7 g

Vegetables and Minced Meat Dog Food

Preparation time: 30 minutes

Cooking time: 0 minutes

Servings: Approximately 15.5 lb

Ingredients:

- 11 lb meat, chopped or minced
- 1.1 lb partially cooked vegetables like carrots, green beans, peas, yam, celery, greens, etc.
- 1.1 lb organ meat

Power Additions:

- 2-3 whole raw eggs

- 1 ½ tbsp oil (choose from cod liver, flax, primrose oil, or hemp oil)
- 1-2 tbsp kelp powder
- 3-4 cups oats (optional)

Directions:

1. You can also use raw vegetables if you do not want to parboil the vegetables.
2. Add the minced meat, organ meat, vegetables, eggs (with shells), oil, kelp powder, and oats into a mixing bowl.
3. Make portions and place them in separate bags or lunch boxes. Keep 1 bag in the refrigerator to use and the rest of the bags in the freezer.
4. Use within 2-3 weeks. Remove one bag from the freezer daily and place it in the refrigerator to thaw.
5. Serve at room temperature or warm.

Nutrition per serving: Calories: 300 kcal; Fat: 15 g; Carbs: 10 g; Protein: 20 g

Beefy Stew

Preparation time: 10 minutes

Cooking time: 20-30 minutes

Servings:

Ingredients:

- ½ cup distilled water
- ½ cup carrots
- 1 lb stew meat (cut into small chunks)
- ¼ cup green beans
- 1 small-medium sweet potato (pre-cooked)
- ¼ cup peas
- 1 tbsp olive oil
- ½ cup flour

Directions:

1. Pour the olive oil into a saucepan, then heat over a medium flame. Add the stew meat and cook until it is done.

2. Turn off the heat, then take off the stew meat from the saucepan. Do not discard the liquid.
3. Dice the carrots, green beans, and peas.
4. Peel the sweet potato's skin off.
5. Reheat the liquid in the pan over a medium-low flame.
6. Whisk in the flour slowly, then stir in the water.
7. Once the mixture is thickened, toss in the remaining ingredients and cook for 15-20 minutes more.
8. Allow to cool, and then serve.

Nutrition per serving: Calories: 365 kcal; Fat: 13.5 g; Carbs: 27 g; Protein: 33 g

Pooch's Sardine Cakes

Preparation time: 10 minutes

Cooking time: 8 minutes

Servings: 6-9 (depending on the sweet potatoes size)

Ingredients:

- 2 (3.75-ounce) sardines cans in water, drained and chopped
- 2 sweet potatoes, cooked
- 1 ½ cup panko breadcrumbs divided
- 2 tbsp all-purpose flour
- 1 egg, beaten

Directions:

1. First, peel the skins from the sweet potatoes; discard the peels.
2. In a huge mixing bowl, mash the sweet potatoes.
3. Add the sardines, flour, and egg to a mixing bowl and combine with the potatoes.
4. Stir into the mixture 1 cup the panko breadcrumbs and mix well.
5. Shape the mixture into 3" patties. Roll your patties in the remaining breadcrumbs to coat.

6. Heat about two tablespoons of olive oil over a medium-high flame in a huge pan.
7. Fry two or three sardine patties for about 8 minutes, flipping patties halfway, until golden brown.
8. Drain the patties on a paper towel and cool them before serving to your pooch.

Keep in your fridge for up to 4 days, place it in an airtight container, and freeze for up to 6 months.

Nutrition per serving: Calories: 150 kcal; Fat: 5 g; Carbs: 20 g; Protein: 8 g

Homemade Recipes for Adult Dogs

Beef Fried Rice

Preparation time: 5 minutes

Cooking time: 20 minutes

Servings: 2

Ingredients:

- ½ cup lean beef chopped
- ½ cup rice
- 1 carrot, chopped
- ⅓ cup spinach
- 6 basil leaves
- 1 tsp sesame oil
- 1 cup water

Directions:

1. In a pot, add the sesame oil.
2. Fry the beef until it is brown.
3. Add the rice, carrot, and toss for 2 minutes.
4. Add one cup of water. Cook for 8 minutes.
5. Add the basil and spinach. Cook until the water evaporates.
6. Serve.

Nutrition per serving: Calories: 350 kcal; Fat: 8 g; Carbs: 45 g; Protein: 20 g

Homemade Beef Stew

Preparation time: 30 minutes

Cooking time: 40 minutes

Servings: 2 servings

Ingredients:

- 1 tbsp vegetable oil
- 2 medium potatoes, chopped
- 1 lb beef
- 2 celery stalks, chopped
- 2 carrots, chopped
- 4 cups chicken stock

Directions:

1. Pour the oil into a skillet and heat.
2. Add the beef to the skillet and brown it.
3. Pour the chicken stock into a pot. Add the celery, potatoes, and carrots. Add the browned beef.
4. Bring the mixture to a boil, lower the heat, then cook for 40 minutes.
5. Allow it to cool, then serve one plate. Reserve the rest for another time.

Nutrition per serving: Calories: 665 kcal; Fat: 28 g; Carbs: 44 g; Protein: 59 g

Beef Broccoli Sweet Potato Rice

Preparation time: 5 minutes

Cooking time: 20 minutes

Servings: 2

Ingredients:

- ½ cup basmati rice
- ⅓ cup sweet potato, cubed
- ⅓ cup broccoli florets, diced
- ½ cup ground beef
- 1 tsp olive oil
- ½ tsp cumin
- ½ tsp basil powder
- 1 cup water

Directions:

1. In a huge pan, add the olive oil.
2. Fry the ground beef until brown.
3. Add the rice, then stir for 2 minutes.
4. Add the cumin and basil powder, then mix.

5. Pour in one water cup and cook for 5 minutes.
6. Add the broccoli and sweet potatoes. Cook for another 8 minutes.
7. Serve.

Nutrition per serving: Calories: 350 kcal; Fat: 12 g; Carbs: 35 g; Protein: 22 g

Chicken and Beef Delight

Preparation time: 30 minutes

Cooking time: 0 minutes

Servings: Approximately 27 lb

Ingredients:

- 5.5 lb chicken thighs, breasts, chopped into pieces
- 3.3 lb ground chicken bones
- 6.6 lb beef hearts and liver
- 5.5 lb ground beef, cheek or stewing
- 2.2 lb yams or sweet potatoes, finely cubed
- 2.2 lb broccoli, finely chopped
- 1.1 lb sunflower meal
- 1. 1 lb linseed meal

Directions:

1. Add chicken thighs or breasts, ground chicken bones, ground beef, organ meat, yam, broccoli, sunflower, and linseed meal into a mixing bowl. Mix until well combined.
2. Make portions and place them in separate bags or lunch boxes. Keep 1 bag in the refrigerator to use and the rest of the bags in the freezer.
3. Use within 2-3 weeks. Remove one bag from the freezer daily and place it in the refrigerator to thaw.
4. Serve at room temperature or warm.

Nutrition per serving: Calories: 500 kcal; Fat: 20 g; Carbs: 20 g; Protein: 60 g

Ground Chicken With Rice & Vegetables

Preparation time: 10 minutes

Cooking time: 55 minutes

Servings: 8 cup dog food

Ingredients:

- 3 cups water
- 1 medium zucchini (peeled & shredded)
- 3 lb ground chicken
- 1 ½ cup fresh spinach (chopped)
- 1 tbsp olive oil
- 1 ½ cup brown or white rice
- 2 carrots (shredded)
- ½ cup fresh peas (frozen & canned will work as long as they are salt-free)
- 1 ½ cup Tuscan kale (chopped)

Directions:

1. Cook your rice in a saucepan according to the instructions on its package. When done, set aside.
2. Pour olive oil into a skillet, then heat over a medium-high fire.
3. Add the ground chicken and fry until brown, for about 5-6 minutes.
4. Add the cooked rice to the pan. Add the fresh vegetables and let them cook until the spinach looks wilted.
5. Allow to cool before serving or storing in your refrigerator.

Nutrition per serving: Calories: 300 kcal; Fat: 12 g; Carbs: 20 g; Protein: 25 g

Easy Turkey and Rice

Preparation time: 5 minutes

Cooking time: 20 minutes

Servings: 4

Ingredients:

- ¼ cup leek, chopped
- 1 cup turkey cubes
- 1 cup rice
- 2 cups turkey broth
- ½ tsp cumin powder
- 1 tsp olive oil

Directions:

1. Add the olive oil to a pot.
2. Stir in the leek and fry until golden.
3. Add the turkey and cook until they are slightly golden.
4. Add the rice, then stir for 2 minutes.
5. Add the cumin and stir for 2 minutes.
6. Pour in the turkey broth and cook until the liquid evaporates. Serve.

Nutrition per serving: Calories: 320 kcal; Fat: 4 g; Carbs: 48 g; Protein: 22 g

Fish and Cornmeal

Preparation time: 20 minutes

Cooking time: 15 minutes

Servings: Approximately 27-28 lb

Ingredients:

- 1 can deboned salmon
- 1 beaten egg
- 3 tbsp cornmeal
- 1 potato
- 1 carrot
- 1 celery stalk
- 1 cup of low-fat yogurt or cottage cheese is approximately 8-8.5 ounces

Directions:

1. Simply combine the salmon, egg, and cornmeal. Form them into patties and press in more cornmeal.
2. Sauté in a pan sprayed with canola until cooked. Steam and chop the vegetables. Cut the salmon into small bites and combine with the vegetables.

3. Add a bit of cottage cheese or yogurt for more texture.

Nutrition per serving: Calories: 120 kcal; Fat: 5 g; Carbs: 5 g; Protein: 13 g

Egg Chicken Meatloaf

Preparation time: 5 minutes

Cooking time: 20 minutes

Servings: 4

Ingredients:

- 2 eggs
- 1 cup chicken, minced
- 2 carrots, chopped
- ½ cup peas
- ½ cup flour
- ½ tsp cinnamon
- ½ tsp basil powder

Directions:

1. Boil the eggs for 5 minutes. Add to a cold bath.
2. Combine the minced chicken, flour, carrot, peas, cinnamon, and basil powder.
3. Add some water to make it stick.
4. Grease a meatloaf tray and add the mixture.
5. Remove the eggshells. Make two sections in the meatloaf tray.
6. Add the boiled eggs. Bake in the oven for 20 minutes at 380°F.
7. Serve.

Nutrition per serving: Calories: 205.5 kcal; Fat: 16 g; Carbs: 16 g; Protein: 14 g

One-Pot Chicken and Squash

Preparation time: 5 minutes

Cooking time: 20 minutes

Servings: 4

Ingredients:

- 4 chicken pieces, boneless
- 1 cup squash, cubed
- ½ cup potatoes, cubed
- 2 tbsp basil, minced
- ½ tsp cumin
- 1 tsp olive oil
- 1 cup chicken broth
- 1 pinch cinnamon

Directions:

1. In a regular pot, add the squash, potatoes, and chicken.
2. Add the basil, cinnamon, and cumin on top.
3. Drizzle in the olive oil.
4. Pour in the chicken broth and cover with a lid.
5. Cook for 20 minutes on medium heat.
6. Serve.

Nutrition per serving: Calories: 300 kcal; Fat: 10 g; Carbs: 15 g; Protein: 35 g

Chickpea Beef Croutons

Preparation time: 5 minutes

Cooking time: 10 minutes

Servings: 10

Ingredients:

- 1 cup boiled chickpeas
- 1 egg
- 1 cup ground beef
- 1 tbsp basil, chopped
- 1 carrot, shredded
- 1 tbsp leek, chopped finely
- 1 tsp olive oil
- ½ tsp cinnamon
- ½ tsp turmeric

Directions:

1. Add the chickpeas to a blender.
2. Blend the mixture until smooth.
3. Add the carrot, beef, leek, basil, cinnamon, turmeric, and egg.
4. Mix well. Make 10 round croutons.
5. Place them on parchment paper on your baking sheet.
6. Add the olive oil on top. Bake for 15 minutes. Serve.

Nutrition per serving: Calories: 85 kcal; Fat: 3 g; Carbs: 6 g; Protein: 7 g

Super Nutritious Dog Bowl

Preparation time: 5 minutes

Cooking time: 20 minutes

Servings: 4

Ingredients:

- ½ cup green gram, boiled
- 2 carrots, roughly chopped
- 1 cup chicken broth
- 1 cup chicken cubes
- ¼ cup green beans, diced
- ½ cup black eyes peas, boiled
- ¼ cup peas
- 1 tsp cinnamon
- ½ tsp turmeric
- 1 tbsp cilantro, chopped
- 1 tbsp basil, chopped
- 1 tsp olive oil

Directions:

1. In a pot, add the olive oil. Fry the chicken cubes for 2 minutes.
2. Add the green grams and black-eyes peas.
3. Stir for 2 minutes. Add cinnamon, turmeric and stir for 1 minute.
4. Pour in the broth. Bring it to a boil.
5. Add the peas, carrots, and green beans.
6. Cook for 8 minutes. Add the basil and cilantro. Remove from heat.

7. Serve.

Nutrition per serving: Calories: 225 kcal; Fat: 4 g; Carbs: 28 g; Protein: 17 g

Turkey, Carrot, Spinach, and Corn

Preparation time: 10 minutes

Cooking time: 15 minutes

Servings: 2

Ingredients:

- ⅔ cup ground turkey
- 1 carrot, chopped
- ¼ cup corn kernels
- ¼ cup spinach
- ½ tsp cumin
- ½ tsp turmeric
- ½ tsp cinnamon
- 1 tsp olive oil

Directions:

1. Heat the olive oil In a pan.
2. Fry the ground turkey for 3 minutes.
3. Add the carrots and stir for 2 minutes.
4. Add turmeric, cumin, and cinnamon. Stir for 1 minute.
5. Add the corn and spinach. Mix well.
6. Cover with a lid and cook on medium-low heat for 3 minutes. Serve.

Nutrition per serving: Calories: 230 kcal; Fat: 10 g; Carbs: 12 g; Protein: 22 g

Doggy Sardine Chicken Kibble

Preparation time: 10 minutes

Cooking time: 90 minutes

Servings: About 2 lb

Ingredients:

- ¾ cup extra-virgin olive oil
- 3 sweet potatoes, baked
- 2 cups nonfat dry milk powder
- 3 eggs
- 1 lb cooked chicken gizzards
- 1 can (3.75-ounce) sardines in water
- 9 ½ cups whole-wheat flour
- 1 ½ cup water, divided

Directions:

1. Preheat your oven to 250°F—lightly oil two baking sheets.
2. Peel your sweet potatoes, and discard the peels. Purée sweet potatoes with ¾ cup water in a food processor. It will make about 2 ½ cups, then set aside.
3. Chop the chicken gizzards finely in your food processor along with ¾ cup water. Add the sardines and blend until smooth.
4. Combine milk powder, olive oil, flour, and eggs in a mixing bowl. Add your sweet potatoes, chopped gizzards, and sardines. Mix well.
5. Prepare the dough on a nice floured surface. Add more flour as needed. Work your dough until you have an even consistency, then roll it out to ¼" to ½" thick.
6. Slice your dough into strips using a pizza cutter, then place it on the prepared baking sheets. Your dough strips should be about ½" apart on the baking sheets.
7. Bake for 45 minutes, then turn your dough strips over. Use your pizza cutter to cut the dough into ½" squares (or you can cut them smaller, depending on the size of your pooch). Return to the baking sheets and bake for another 45 minutes.
8. Turn off your oven. Flip the squares using a spatula and ensure they are not touching. Return the baking sheet to the oven, then allow to cool.
9. Once the kibble is cooled, store it for 1 week in the fridge. Place the remaining kibble in an airtight container and store it in the freezer for up 6 months.

Nutrition per serving: Calories: 280 kcal; Fat: 10 g; Carbs: 35 g; Protein: 12 g

Rover's Deviled Eggs

Preparation time: 10 minutes

Cooking time: 10 minutes

Servings: 12 deviled eggs

Ingredients:

- ¼ cup cooked and puréed chicken livers
- water as needed
- 6 eggs
- 1 tsp organic apple cider vinegar

Directions:

1. Add your eggs to a pot filled with water and boil for 3 minutes on a low fire.
2. Remove the eggs from the heat and keep the lid on the pot for about 15 minutes.
3. Uncover the eggs and rinse them under cold water.
4. Crack and peel the eggs under running water, then set them aside.
5. Slice your eggs lengthwise, remove the yolks, and place them in a bowl.
6. Add your chicken liver purée to the bowl along with the apple cider vinegar.
7. Mash your egg yolks, chicken livers, and apple cider vinegar into a fine crumble.
8. Add the mixture to the egg whites and serve to your furry pal!

Nutrition per serving: Calories: 84 kcal; Fat: 5.4 g; Carbs: 0.6 g; Protein: 7.5 g

Mixed Chicken, Pork, and Beef Raw Dog Food

Preparation time: 30 minutes

Cooking time: 0 minutes

Servings: Approximately 24.25 lb

Ingredients:

- 5.5 lb fresh Irish chicken mince with 15% bone
- 5.5 lb fresh Irish duck mince with 15% bone
- 2.2 lb beef or beef and pork liver mixture
- 1.1 lb beef or a beef and pork heart mix
- 1.1 lb beef or a beef and pork kidney mixture
- 2.2 lb frozen vegetables (mixture of peas, green beans, and carrots)
- 5.5 lb fatty Irish beef mince
- 2.2 lb boiled brown rice
- 3 free-range eggs

Directions:

1. Add the minced meat, organ meat, vegetables, eggs, oil, and boiled rice into a mixing bowl. Mix until well combined.
2. Make portions and place them in separate bags or lunch boxes. Keep 1 bag in the refrigerator to use and the rest of the bags in the freezer.
3. Use within 2-3 weeks. Remove one bag from the freezer daily and place it in the refrigerator to thaw.
4. Serve at room temperature or warm.
5. Note: To increase the calories in the food, replace the chicken with the equivalent amount of duck mince. You can also increase the quantity of brown rice.
6. To reduce calories, replace red meat with equivalent chicken, fish, or turkey mince.

Nutrition per serving: Calories: 321 kcal; Fat: 12 g; Carbs: 13 g; Protein: 21 g

Turkey Fried Rice

Preparation time: 5 minutes

Cooking time: 20 minutes

Servings: 2

Ingredients:

- 1 egg
- 1 tsp olive oil
- ½ cup basmati rice
- 1 tbsp leek, chopped
- ¼ cup peas
- 1 carrot, thinly shredded
- ½ cup ground turkey
- ½ tsp cinnamon
- ½ tsp turmeric
- ½ tsp cumin
- 1 cup water

Directions:

1. In a huge pan, heat the olive oil and fry the ground turkey for 2 minutes.
2. Add the leek and toss for 1 minute.
3. Add the rice and spices, and stir for 1 minute.
4. Pour in 1 cup water. Cook for 8 minutes.
5. Break in the egg, add the peas and carrot.
6. Cook for 5 minutes. Serve.

Nutrition per serving: Calories: 380 kcal; Fat: 10 g; Carbs: 42 g; Protein: 26 g

Lamb Doggy Hash

Preparation time: 10 minutes

Cooking time: 10 minutes

Servings: 7 cups

Ingredients:

- 1 lb ground lamb
- 2 tbsp olive oil
- 1 cup low-fat plain yogurt
- 1 cup frozen mixed vegetables (no onions)
- 2 cups white rice, cooked
- 2 cups brown rice, cooked

Directions:

1. Heat your olive oil in a skillet over a medium-high fire. Cook the ground lamb until no longer pink, then drain off excess fat.
2. Add the mixed vegetables, and stir, then remove from heat.
3. Mix your lamb, yogurt, and rice in a large mixing bowl.
4. Cool the mixture before serving to your furry pal.
5. Keep the mixture in your fridge for up to 3 days, or place it in an airtight container and freeze for up to 6 months.

Nutrition per serving: Calories: 435 kcal; Fat: 25 g; Carbs: 31 g; Protein: 21 g

Fido's Stuffed Pumpkin

Preparation time: 5 minutes

Cooking time: 1 hour

Servings: 10 cups

Ingredients:

- 2 tbsp parmesan cheese, grated
- 1 (3lb) cooking pumpkin, seeds removed
- 1 cup green beans, cooked
- 1 apple, cored, seeds removed
- ½ lb ground turkey or ground chicken

Directions:

1. Preheat your oven to 350°F.
2. Take off the top of the pumpkin; using a large spoon remove all the seeds.
3. Next, core your apples and discard the core and seeds. Finely chop the apple.
4. Chop the green beans, then add into a mixing bowl along with the apple, Parmesan cheese, and turkey (or other meat of your choice). Mix well.
5. Add the mixture into the pumpkin cavity and place the pumpkin onto a baking sheet.

6. Set your baking sheet on the middle rack of your oven and bake for 1 hour.
7. Drain any liquid that may accumulate on the top of the pumpkin during baking.
8. Cool the pumpkin entirely before serving it to your furry friend. You can save unused portions in your fridge for up to 3 days, place them in an airtight container, and then freeze them for up to 2 months.

Nutrition per serving: Calories: 113 kcal; Fat: 3.1 g; Carbs: 12.4 g; Protein: 9.5 g

Raw Meatloaf

Preparation time: 15 minutes

Cooking time: 0 minutes

Servings: 6 cups

Ingredients:

- 3 eggs with shells, finely broken
- 2 cups puréed vegetables
- 1 lb raw ground beef, turkey, or chicken
- ½ cup organic apple cider vinegar
- ¼ cup liver or kidneys rinsed
- ½ cup low-fat plain yogurt

Directions:

1. Add all ingredients into a mixing bowl. Combine well. Serve.
2. Keep it in the refrigerator for 3 days or store it in a sealed container in the freezer for a maximum of 6 months.

Nutrition per serving: Calories: 200 kcal; Fat: 10 g; Carbs: 5 g; Protein: 15 g

Fishermen's Eggs

Preparation time: 10 minutes

Cooking time: 10-15 minutes

Servings: 2 cups

Ingredients:

- 2 tbsp fresh parsley
- 1 (3.75 oz) can sardines in water
- 4 eggs

Directions:

1. Prepare the oven to 375°F. Grease with nonstick cooking spray an 8 X 8 casserole dish that can go in the oven.
2. Drain the sardines. Use sardine water as a nice topping for your dog's meal. Chop the sardines and mix them with the parsley.
3. Cover the bottom of the dish with the sardine mixture, then crack the eggs and put them on top.
4. Bake for 10 to 15 minutes until the eggs reach the desired level of doneness.
5. Wait until the food is cool before giving it to your dog. Refrigerate for up to 3 days or freeze in a sealed container for up to 6 months, depending on your preference.

Nutrition per serving: Calories: 320 kcal; Fat: 22 g; Carbs: 2 g; Protein: 26 g

Turkey Gravy

Preparation time: 5 minutes

Cooking time: 10 minutes

Servings: About 2 cups

Ingredients:

- ¼ cup all-purpose flour
- 2 cups pan drippings
- 1 cup cooked and shredded turkey meat
- ¼ cup water

Directions:

1. Let the drippings cool, then skim the fat off it. Set aside ¼ cup of fat.
2. Heat the reserved fat in a large skillet over a medium-high fire. Add flour.

3. Stir constantly until the flour is brown, about a minute. Pour in drippings and water, stirring continuously and reducing to desired thickness.
4. Add the shredded turkey meat to the sauce and stir until well combined.
5. Allow to cool completely before serving. Keep it in the refrigerator for up to 3 days or store it in a sealed container in the freezer for up to 6 months.

Nutrition per serving: Calories: 150 kcal; Fat: 10 g; Carbs: 8 g; Protein: 2 g

Baked Egg Cup

Preparation time: 10 minutes

Cooking time: 25-30 minutes

Servings: 16 mini-muffins

Ingredients:

- ½ tsp baking powder
- 1 can (5-ounce) tuna in water, drained
- 8 eggs
- ½ cup shredded cooked chicken
- ½ cup cottage cheese
- 1 cup shredded cheddar cheese

Directions:

1. Preheat your oven to 350°F.
2. Using a parchment cup, line a mini-muffin tin.
3. Crack the eggs into a big bowl and whisk. Add cottage cheese, chicken, baking powder, tuna, and cheese. Combine well.
4. Fill each parchment cup with ⅔ of the egg mixture. Bake in the oven for 25-30 minutes.
5. Allow cooling before serving. Keep it in the refrigerator for up to 3 days.

Nutrition per serving: Calories: 91 kcal; Fat: 6 g; Carbs: 0.5 g; Protein: 8 g

Chili Cheese Bake Homemade Dog Food

Preparation time: 30 minutes

Cooking time: 30 minutes

Servings: 4 servings

Ingredients:

- 1 lb lean ground beef or turkey
- 1 cup cooked brown rice
- 1 cup chopped carrots
- 1 cup chopped green beans
- 1 cup low-sodium beef or chicken broth
- ¼ cup canned pumpkin (not pumpkin pie filling)
- ¼ cup grated low-fat cheddar cheese
- ¼ cup grated low-fat mozzarella cheese
- 2 tbsp olive oil
- 1 tsp dried parsley
- ½ tsp dried oregano
- Salt and pepper to taste

Directions:

1. Preheat your oven to 350°F.
2. In a large skillet, heat the olive oil over a medium-high fire. Add the ground beef or turkey and cook until browned about 5-7 minutes. Drain any excess fat.
3. Add the chopped carrots and green beans to the skillet and cook for 5 minutes or until the vegetables are tender.
4. Combine the cooked rice, beef, or chicken broth, canned pumpkin, dried parsley, dried oregano, salt, and pepper in a mixing bowl.
5. Add the ground beef or turkey mixture to the mixing bowl and stir to combine.
6. Transfer the mixture to a casserole dish and sprinkle the grated cheddar and mozzarella cheese.
7. Bake for 20-25 minutes or until the cheese is melted and bubbly.

8. Allow to cool before serving to your dog.

Nutrition per serving: Calories: 290 kcal; Fat: 10 g; Carbs: 24 g; Protein: 24 g

Liver Gravy

Preparation time: 10 minutes

Cooking time: 15 minutes

Servings: 3–4 cups

Ingredients:

- 1 lb chicken liver, rinsed
- 2 cups chicken broth
- 1 tbsp olive oil

Directions:

1. Over medium-high heat, cook the liver in oil in a fairly large skillet until brown.
2. Transfer the liver to a food processor. Add the chicken broth and process until pureed.
3. You can refrigerate it for 3 days or freeze it for up to 6 months in a sealed container.

Nutrition per serving: Calories: 160 kcal; Fat: 8 g; Carbs: 5 g; Protein: 16 g

Mixed Olive, Canola, Cod Liver, and Flax Seed Oil Supplement

Preparation time: 15 minutes

Cooking time: 0 minutes

Servings: Approximately 22 lb

Ingredients:

- ¼ cup olive oil
- ¼ cup canola oil
- ¼ cup cod liver oil
- ¼ cup flax seed oil

Directions:

1. Place the oils in a brown bottle and shake well.
2. Refrigerate.
3. Add two teaspoons to the dog food each day. It can be added to dry food as well.
4. Safflower and Sunflower oil may be used as well.

Nutrition per serving: Calories: 85 kcal; Fat: 1 g; Carbs: 4 g; Protein: 8 g

Pumpkin Pudding for Doggies

Preparation time: 40 minutes

Cooking time: 0 minutes

Servings: Approximately 24 lb

Ingredients:

- 1 lb raw beef mince
- 1 cup raw pumpkin, puree
- 1 cup raw carrot, puree
- 2 tbsp extra virgin coconut oil
- ¼ cup ground flaxseeds
- ¼ cup ground sunflower seeds
- Coconut flour to dust
- 4 raspberries to garnish
- 4 blueberries to garnish

Directions:

1. Add raw pumpkin cubes into the food processor and process until smooth. Measure 1 cup of the pureed pumpkin and add into a mixing bowl.
2. Add raw carrot cubes into the food processor and process until smooth. Measure 1 cup of the pureed carrot and add it to the bowl of pumpkin.
3. Add beef mince and mix until well combined.
4. Add coconut oil and mix until well combined.
5. Add ground flax seeds and sunflower seeds and stir until well combined. You

can use your hands to combine the mixture.

6. Fill into 4 ramekins or teacups. Press it well onto the bottom of the cup. Chill for 30-40 minutes.
7. Remove from the refrigerator and invert onto a plate. Tap the bottom of the cup to loosen the pudding.
8. Dust the pudding with coconut flour. Garnish with a raspberry and a blueberry on each pudding and serve.
9. Place individual portions in separate containers and place them in the refrigerator.

Nutrition per serving: Calories: 254 kcal; Fat: 23.5 g; Carbs: 6.9 g; Protein: 6.4 g

Homemade Chicken, Sweet Potatoes, and Kale

Preparation time: 30 minutes

Cooking time: 60 minutes

Servings: 3 weeks of food

Ingredients:

- 2 cups brown rice
- 2 chicken thighs, shredded
- 2 chicken breasts, shredded
- 1 ½ cup kale, chopped
- 1 sweet potato, peeled and diced

Directions:

1. Place the shredded chicken breasts in a bowl. Add brown rice, kale, and sweet potato.
2. Pour some water and let it simmer for 50-60 minutes.
3. Drain any liquid and set it on a sheet pan to dry.
4. Serve. Keep leftovers in the refrigerator or freezer.

Nutrition per serving: Calories: 667 kcal; Fat: 10 g; Carbs: 96 g; Protein: 50 g

Apple and Chicken Broth Frozen Treats

Preparation time: 20 minutes

Cooking time: 0 minutes

Servings: Approximately 15 lb

Ingredients:

- 1 ½ lb apples, cored and sliced
- 32 oz chicken broth, organic

Directions:

1. Prepare the apple slices by chopping them into bite-sized pieces.
2. Divide the prepared apples between an ice tray or Jell-O shot container.
3. Fill each ice tray opening or container with the chicken broth, leaving a small room at the top. If using a Jell-O shot container, secure the lid onto it before continuing.
4. Freeze the treats in the freezer for at least 4 hours.
5. Once frozen, remove the ice tray from the freezer and pop the treats out. Store in an airtight container or Ziploc bag in the freezer. Jell-O shot containers can stay in the freezer until ready to use.

Nutrition per serving: Calories: 31 kcal; Fat: 0.2 g; Carbs: 6.4 g; Protein: 0.9 g

Beef and Greens for Beginners

Preparation time: 40 minutes

Cooking time: 0 minutes

Servings: Approximately 28 lb

Ingredients:

- 1 1 lb ground, cheek, or stewing beef
- 3.3 lb beef tail bones
- 6.6 lb beef hearts and liver

- 2.2 lb celery, finely chopped
- 1.1 lb collard greens, finely chopped
- 2.2 lb green apples, finely chopped
- 4 lb kale, discard hard ribs and stems, finely chopped
- 3 chicken eggs, lightly boiled

Directions:

1. Add the meat, organ meat, tailbones, eggs (with their shells), apples, celery, collard greens, and kale into a mixing bowl. Mix until well combined.
2. Make portions and place them in separate bags or lunch boxes. Keep 1 bag in the refrigerator to use and the rest of the bags in the freezer.
3. Use within 2-3 weeks. Remove one bag from the freezer daily and place it in the refrigerator to thaw.
4. Serve at room temperature or warm.

Nutrition per serving: Calories: 265 kcal; Fat: 13 g; Carbs: 8 g; Protein: 23 g

Rover's Raw Chicken Dinner

Preparation time: 5 minutes

Cooking time: 0 minutes

Servings: 3 cups

Ingredients:

- 2 whole chicken livers, rinsed and chopped
- 1 lb raw chicken, chopped
- 1 tsp alfalfa powder
- 1 egg
- 1 tsp kelp seaweed powder
- 1 tbsp organic apple cider vinegar
- ½ tsp flaxseed oil
- 1 tsp raw honey
- 2 ½ tbsp low-fat plain yogurt
- ½ garlic clove, chopped

Directions:

1. Combine the ingredients in a mixing bowl using a large spoon, then portion the meal based on your pet's size.
2. Place the mixture in your fridge for up to 3 days, or freeze it in an airtight container for about 6 months.

Nutrition per serving: Calories: 230 kcal; Fat: 12 g; Carbs: 6 g; Protein: 25 g

Meat and Grain Menu

Preparation time: 15 minutes

Cooking time: 0 minutes

Servings: Approximately 2 servings

Ingredients:

- 2 cups brown rice cooked
- ⅔ cup lean meat
- ¼ cup vegetables grated, no onion
- 2 tsp lard or veggie oil

Directions:

1. Mix all ingredients.
2. Serve slightly warm.

Nutrition per serving: Calories: 130 kcal; Fat: 36 g; Carbs: 130 g; Protein: 56 g

Banana and Strawberry Frozen Smoothie Dog Treats

Preparation time: 20 minutes

Cooking time: 0 minutes

Servings: Approximately 12 servings

Ingredients:

- 1 ½ cup low-fat Greek yogurt, plain
- 2 cups strawberries, destemmed and sliced
- 1 banana, peeled and sliced
- 3 tbsp honey

- ¼ cup skim milk

Directions:

1. Put all the ingredients into a blender. On medium speed, blend the mixture for several minutes until smooth.
2. Pour the blended mixture into the desired molds. Molds shaped like a bone work great, but any mold will do.
3. Place the mold in the freezer and let it freeze for at least 4 hours.
4. Once the treats are completely frozen, pop them out of the mold. Store the treats in an airtight container or Ziploc bag in the freezer. These treats can be stored for up to 2 months with proper storage.

Nutrition per serving: Calories: 25 kcal; Fat: 1 g; Carbs: 4 g; Protein: 2 g

Lamb/Beef, Vegetable, and Fruit for Small Breed Dogs up to 17.5 Lb

Preparation time: 25 minutes

Cooking time: 0 minutes

Servings: Approximately 2-2 ½ lb

Ingredients:

- 1.1 lb lamb or beef, chopped
- 2 apples, cored, chopped
- 3 cups pumpkin or squash, chopped
- 2 large carrots, chopped (about 2 cups)
- ½ cup frozen peas, thawed
- 1 ⅓ cup brown or basmati rice
- 3 cups water or unsalted broth without onion
- 2 tsp fish oil
- 8 tsp sunflower oil
- other ingredients: to be added at each feed
- 1 Cenovis tablets (zinc tablets)
- ⅛ tsp iodized salt
- 1 trace nutrients copper plus tablet (2 mg)
- 1 Centrum advance multivitamin / multi-mineral supplement

Directions:

1. Add rice, broth, or water and pumpkin into a saucepan. Cook until very tender. Turn off the heat and cool completely.
2. Add meat, apple, pumpkin, carrots, peas, rice, fish oil, and sunflower oil into a mixing bowl. Mix until well combined.
3. Make portions and place them in separate bags or lunch boxes. Keep 1 bag in the refrigerator to use and the rest of the bags in the freezer.
4. Use within 2-3 weeks. Remove one bag from the freezer daily and place it in the refrigerator to thaw.
5. Serve at room temperature or warm.
6. Add Cenovis tablet, salt, copper plus tablet, and Centrum in each feed while serving.

Nutrition per serving: Calories: 350 kcal; Fat: 14 g; Carbs: 36 g; Protein: 20 g

Lentil Loaves

Preparation time: 15 minutes

Cooking time: 25 minutes

Servings: 8 muffins

Ingredients:

- ¼ cup shredded carrots
- 1 cup dry lentils
- 1 cup old-fashioned oats
- 1 egg

Directions:

1. Preheat your oven to 350°F. Line a muffin tin with a parchment cup.
2. Cook your lentils according to the instructions on their package. When done, drain the water and pour it into a

bowl, then use a potato masher to mash them.

3. Allow to cool. When cool, add oats, carrots, and eggs. Stir until the mixture is well combined.
4. Fill the lined muffin cup with the mixture about two-thirds full.
5. Bake in the oven for 20-25 minutes.
6. Allow cooling before serving. Keep it in the refrigerator for 5 days or store it in a sealed container in the freezer for up to 6 months.

Nutrition per serving: Calories: 130 kcal; Fat: 1.5 g; Carbs: 23 g; Protein: 8 g

Beef and Eggs

Preparation time: 20 minutes

Cooking time: 0minutes

Servings: Approximately 12 lb

Ingredients:

- 5 lb raw ground beef
- 7-8 cups cooked white rice, cooled
- 9 hard-boiled eggs with shells, cooled
- Dinovite daily dog supplement (follow the instructions on the package and use accordingly or use one tablespoon per cup of the recipe)
- 2 LickOchopstubes

Directions:

1. Add ground beef, white rice, and eggs into a mixing bowl. Mix until well combined.
2. Make portions and place them in separate bags or lunch boxes. Keep 1 bag in the refrigerator to use and the rest of the bags in the freezer.
3. Use within 2-3 weeks. Remove one bag from the freezer daily and place it in the refrigerator to thaw.
4. Serve at room temperature or warm.

5. Follow the instructions on the packages of Dinovite and LickOchops and add them to the portion while serving.
6. Note: Please do not give it to your dog without Dinovite and LickOchops.

Nutrition per serving: Calories: 125 kcal; Fat: 1 g; Carbs: 1 g; Protein: 1 g

Homemade Doggie Donut Snacks

Preparation time: 30 minutes

Cooking time: 20 minutes

Servings: 2 dozen

Ingredients:

- ½ cup skim milk
- 1 egg
- ¼ cup carob powder
- 1 cup wheat flour
- ¼ cup water
- 1 tbsp baking powder
- ½ cup peanut butter

Directions:

1. Crack the egg into a bowl, then whisk. Add the milk and peanut and mix well.
2. Add the wheat flour and baking powder. Stir well.
3. Dust a clean surface with flour. Roll the batter onto the floured surface.
4. Cut into round shapes and remove the center.
5. Place them in the oven, then bake for 15-20 minutes at 375°F.
6. In the meantime, add water to a bowl and combine it with carob powder.
7. When the donut is ready, retrieve it from the oven and allow it to cool. Then, frost with the water and carob mixture when cooled.
8. Keep them in a sealed container.

Nutrition per serving: Calories: 105 kcal; Fat: 3.5 g; Carbs: 14 g; Protein: 4 g

Homemade Sweet Potato Chews

Preparation time: 15 minutes

Cooking time: 3 hours

Servings: 12 chews

Ingredients:

- 2 sliced sweet potatoes

Directions:

1. Slice the potatoes into thin pieces.
2. Using parchment paper, line a cookie sheet. Arrange the sweet potatoes neatly on it.
3. Place them in the oven and bake at 250°F for 3 hours, flipping halfway through.
4. Store the potato chews in the refrigerator.

Nutrition per serving: Calories: 28 kcal; Fat: 0.5 g; Carbs: 6.5 g; Protein: 0.5 g

Salmon and Spinach Hash

Preparation time: 10 minutes

Cooking time: 15 minutes

Servings: 4 cups

Ingredients:

- 1 can (7.5-ounce) drained salmon
- 1 tsp olive oil
- 4 eggs
- 1 cup frozen spinach, thawed

Directions:

1. Pour olive oil into a skillet, then heat over a medium-high flame. Add spinach and salmon, stirring continuously until the mixture is heated.
2. Add the eggs and scramble them.

3. Allow to cool, and then serve. Keep it in the refrigerator for up to 3 days.

Nutrition per serving: Calories: 215 kcal; Fat: 12 g; Carbs: 3 g; Protein: 23 g

Chickpea Stew

Preparation time: 15 minutes

Cooking time: 6 hours

Servings: 9 cups

Ingredients:

- 1 cup (¼" -thick) carrot slices
- 1 cup light coconut milk
- 1 tbsp olive oil
- 1 tsp peeled and grated fresh ginger
- 1 cup green beans, chopped
- 1 tsp brown sugar
- 1 ¾ cup vegetable stock
- 2 garlic cloves, minced
- 1 ½ cup peeled and cubed baking potato
- 1 (14.5-ounce) can diced tomatoes, undrained
- 3 cups cooked chickpeas
- 1 cup diced green bell pepper
- 3 cups fresh baby spinach

Directions:

1. Pour olive oil into a skillet. Allow it to heat over a medium-high flame. Add the carrot slices and cook until soft. Stir in ginger, brown sugar, and garlic. Cook for 1-2 minutes, stirring regularly to prevent it from clinging. Take off from the heat.
2. Transfer the mixture to a 5-quart slow cooker. Add vegetable stock, potato, tomatoes, chickpeas, bell pepper, and green beans. Cook on high until vegetables become soft, about 6 hours.
3. Add coconut milk and spinach, stirring until the spinach wilts. Allow cooling before serving. Keep it in the refrigerator for up to 3 days.

Nutrition per serving: Calories: 220 kcal; Fat: 6 g; Carbs: 35 g; Protein: 9 g

Chicken and Fish Exotica

Preparation time: 45 minutes

Cooking time: 0 minutes

Servings: Approximately 35 lb

Ingredients:

- 5 lb chicken hearts
- 20 lb chicken necks without skin
- 2 ½ -5 lb chicken liver
- 4 cans Alaskan wild pink salmon (optional)
- 1-2 ½ lb carrots, cut into small pieces
- 1 small beet, cut into small pieces
- 1 lb spinach or any other greens your dog prefers
- 2 cups red cabbage, finely chopped
- 1 apple, cored, cut into small pieces
- ½ cup raw pumpkin seeds (pepitas)

Other Ingredients: Use 2-3 of these

- 2-6 raw eggs
- ½ cup tahini
- 1 cup extra virgin olive oil
- 4-8 tbsp dried oregano
- 4-8 tbsp dried parsley
- 2 tbsp honey
- 2-4 tbspThorvin kelp powder
- 2 tbsp turmeric powder
- ¼ tsp vitamin C powder

Directions:

1. Using a meat grinder, grind the chicken hearts, chicken liver, chicken neck, carrots, beet, spinach, red cabbage, apple, and pepitas into a mixing bowl.
2. Add the rest of the ingredients, then mix until well combined.
3. Make portions and place them in separate bags or lunch boxes. Keep 1 bag in the refrigerator to use and the rest of the bags in the freezer.
4. Use within 2-3 weeks. Remove one bag from the freezer daily and place it in the refrigerator to thaw.
5. Serve at room temperature or warm.

Nutrition per serving: Calories: 220 kcal; Fat: 15 g; Carbs: 20 g; Protein: 32 g

Pressure Cooker Homemade Dog Food

Preparation time: 30 minutes

Cooking time: 60 minutes

Servings: 5 meals

Ingredients:

- Water
- 2 carrots, chopped
- 2 frozen chicken breasts
- 1 sweet potato, chopped
- 2 cups white rice

Directions:

1. Pour water into a pot. Add the chicken breasts and cook for 30 minutes at high pressure.
2. In the meantime, wash the white rice and soak it.
3. When the chicken breasts are cooked, release the steam, then add the remaining ingredients.
4. Cook for 10 minutes under high pressure.
5. Allow to sit for 20 minutes, then shred the chicken. Combine well.
6. Let it cool, and then serve. Store the remaining food in the refrigerator or freezer.

Nutrition per serving: Calories: 465 kcal; Fat: 4.8 g; Carbs: 65 g; Protein: 39 g

Chicken Jerky

Preparation time: 10 minutes

Cooking time: 2 minutes

Servings: 12 strips

Ingredients:

- 1 lb chicken breasts, deboned

Directions:

1. Preheat your oven to 170°F.
2. Grease a cookie sheet with a small edge lightly.
3. Slice the deboned chicken breasts into strips about ¼ inch thick. Arrange the slices neatly on a cookie sheet with about ½ inch of space between them.
4. Place them in the oven and bake for 2 hours. If the slices aren't dry after 2 hours, keep baking.
5. Retrieve them from the oven and let them cool completely, then serve. Keep leftovers in the refrigerator for 3 days or store them in a sealed container for up to 6 months.

Nutrition per serving: Calories: 24 kcal; Fat: 0.4 g; Carbs: 0 g; Protein: 5 g

Homemade Recipes for Senior Dog

Organic Chicken Wings and Carrots

Preparation time: 20 minutes

Cooking time: 0 minutes

Servings: Approximately 4-5

Ingredients:

- ½ cup organic cottage cheese
- ½ cup organic grated carrots
- 4-5 organic skin on raw chicken wings

Directions:

1. Simply mix all these ingredients in your dog's bowl.
2. When preparing homemade food for your dogs, remember that all food must be served at room temperature.
3. If there are any leftovers, keep them stored in the refrigerator in tightly sealed containers for up to four days. It might be better to freeze all food and only thaw certain servings per meal.
4. The easiest way to add a spin to your recipes is to use different base ingredients like turkey, chicken, or beef.
5. Complete meals usually consist of 2 parts protein, 1 part carbohydrates, and 1 part vegetables.
6. You can come up with various recipes with this formula, and your dog will probably love them.

Nutrition per serving: Calories: 141 kcal; Fat: 5 g; Carbs: 8 g; Protein: 14 g

Homemade Organic Stew Dog Food

Preparation time: 15 minutes

Cooking time: 6 hours

Servings: 10 cups

Ingredients:

- 1 large sweet potato, peeled and diced
- 1 cup brown rice
- 1 bag frozen mixed vegetables
- 3 chicken breasts
- 2 ½ cups water

Directions:

1. Add all ingredients into a crock pot. Combine well.
2. Cook for 6 hours.
3. Drain off any liquid and put them in bags, one cup for each bag.

Nutrition per serving: Calories: 160 kcal; Fat: 2 g; Carbs: 20 g; Protein: 15 g

Liver-Bacon Homemade Dog Treats

Preparation time: 30 minutes

Cooking time: 60 minutes

Servings: 40 chews

Ingredients:

- 13 oz beef liver, cut into small pieces
- 1 lb bacon, cooked and drained
- 3 ¼ cups wheat flour
- 1 ¾ tbsp cornmeal
- 1 cup beef stock

Directions:

1. Cook the liver.
2. Add the drained bacon to a food processor. Pulse, then add the cooked liver and cornmeal. Pulse again.
3. Add wheat flour and pulse again.
4. Pour in the beef stock and mix well.

5. Roll out the batter in a rectangular shape. Cut into small squares.
6. Arrange them neatly on a cookie sheet. Place them in the oven, then bake for 50-60 minutes at 350°F.
7. Keep in a container for a maximum of 2 weeks.

Nutrition per serving: Calories: 73 kcal; Fat: 3 g; Carbs: 7 g; Protein: 4 g

Meat, Fruit, and Vegetable Patties

Preparation time: 30 minutes

Cooking time: 0 minutes

Servings: Approximately 6 lb

Ingredients:

- ½ pound chicken livers
- 5 lb ground beef
- 2 small apples, cored, chopped
- 2 carrots, chopped
- 1 cup baby spinach, chopped
- 1 cup plain yogurt
- 2 tbsp olive oil
- 4 whole eggs, lightly boiled
- 2 tbsp ground flaxseed

Directions:

1. Add the fruit and vegetables into a food processor bowl and pulse until the mixture is finely chopped.
2. Add the chicken liver, yogurt, olive oil, eggs, flaxseed, and pulse until well incorporated.
3. Move the mixture into a mixing bowl. Add the beef and mix until well incorporated.
4. Shape into patties of about 3-4 inches in diameter.
5. Line 2 baking sheets with parchment paper. Place the patties on the baking sheet next to each other.

6. Place the baking trays in the freezer and freeze until firm.
7. Make portions and place them in separate bags or lunch boxes. Keep 1 bag in the refrigerator to use and the rest of the bags in the freezer.
8. Use within 2-3 weeks. Remove one bag from the freezer daily and place it in the refrigerator to thaw.
9. Serve at room temperature or warm.

Nutrition per serving: Calories: 255 kcal; Fat: 17 g; Carbs: 6 g; Protein: 21 g

Dehydrated Sweet Potato Chews

Preparation time: 10 minutes

Cooking time: 14 hours

Servings: 18–25 chews

Ingredients:

- 2 medium sweet potatoes

Directions:

1. Remove and discard any sprouts and green spots from the potatoes. Wash and peel the potatoes.
2. Slice the potatoes lengthwise about ¼ inch thick.
3. Set the slices neatly on the dehydrating trays, leaving space between them so the edges can dry properly.
4. Dry the potatoes for about 14 hours (although this will vary by dehydrator).
5. Allow to cool and keep them in the refrigerator for up to 1 week or store them in a sealed container in the freezer for up to 6 months.
6. Note: Dehydrating time may vary depending on the dehydrator.

Nutrition per serving: Calories: 26 kcal; Fat: 0.5 g; Carbs: 6 g; Protein: 0.5 g

Frozen Yogurt Cubes

Preparation time: 10 minutes

Cooking time: 0 minutes

Servings: Approximately 12

Ingredients:

- 6 oz low-fat plain yogurt
- 1 cup sugar-free fruit juice
- ½ cup minced carrots

Directions:

1. Combine all ingredients in a bowl.
2. Spoon the mixture into ice cube trays, then freeze until totally solid.

Nutrition per serving: Calories: 6 kcal; Fat: 0 g; Carbs: 1.5 g; Protein: 0.3 g

Rice and Cheese

Preparation time: 15 minutes

Cooking time: 0 minutes

Servings: Approximately 4 servings

Ingredients:

- ¼ cup cheddar cheese grated
- 2 tbsp safflower oil
- ½ cup rice krispies
- ¼ cup Swiss cheese grated

Directions:

1. Combine the cheese and oil.
2. Using a plastic wrapper, wrap the mixture into a cylinder (1-inch diameter by 7 inches length)
3. Roll in Rice Krispies.
4. Refrigerate.
5. Slice into ½ inch and serve.

Nutrition per serving: Calories: 21 kcal; Fat: 5 g; Carbs: 6 g; Protein: 12 g

Sweet Potato Potstickers

Preparation time: 20 minutes

Cooking time: 20 minutes

Servings: 12 potstickers

Ingredients:

- 1 tbsp sunflower oil
- 1 tbsp fresh rosemary
- 1 cup cooked sweet potato (roughly 2 medium sweet potatoes, peeled)
- ¼ cup grated parmesan cheese
- ⅓ cup ricotta cheese
- 12 wonton wrappers

Directions:

1. Preheat your oven to 350°F.
2. Add the sweet potato, cheese, and rosemary to a food processor. Process until well blended.
3. Place one tablespoon of the sweet potato mixture in the center of a wonton wrapper. Using olive oil, wet the edges of the wrapper and close it. Do the same for the remaining wontons until all filling is used, then arrange the wonton neatly on a baking sheet.
4. Baste the wantons with sunflower oil.
5. Place it in the oven, then bake until golden brown or for 15-20 minutes.
6. Allow to cool, and then serve. You can refrigerate it for 3 days or freeze it for up to 6 months in a sealed container.

Nutrition per serving: Calories: 110 kcal; Fat: 3 g; Carbs: 16 g; Protein: 5 g

Chicken and Carrots for Beginners

Preparation time: 20 minutes

Cooking time: 30 minutes

Servings: Approximately 25.3 lb

Ingredients:

- 6.6 lb chicken heart and liver
- 11 lb chicken thighs or breasts
- 3.3 lb ground chicken bone
- 2.2 lb organic green beans, finely chopped
- 2.2 lb organic carrots, finely chopped
- 3 chicken eggs, lightly boiled

Directions:

1. Add chicken thighs or breasts, ground chicken bone, organ meat, beans, carrots, and eggs (with shells) into a mixing bowl. Mix until well combined.
2. Make portions and place them in separate bags or lunch boxes. Keep 1 bag in the refrigerator to use and the rest of the bags in the freezer.
3. Use within 2-3 weeks. Remove one bag from the freezer daily and place it in the refrigerator to thaw.
4. Serve at room temperature or warm.

Nutrition per serving: Calories: 365 kcal; Fat: 15 g; Carbs: 5 g; Protein: 44 g

Happy Barks Meatloaf Meal

Preparation time: 10 minutes

Cooking time: 1 hour

Servings: 16 cups

Ingredients:

- 4 large eggs
- 4 lb lean ground turkey
- 2 cups puréed green beans, steamed
- 2 cups puréed potatoes, steamed
- 2 cups puréed carrots, steamed
- ½ lb organic beef liver or chicken liver, rinsed and diced.

Directions:

1. To begin, heat your oven to 350°F.

2. Combine all the ingredients and divide them into four 8"x 4" loaf pans. Each loaf pan should be about ¾ full.
3. Bake the mixture for an hour. Drain off any excess grease.
4. Cool and keep in the fridge 1 week's worth of dog food.
5. Place the remaining food inside a zip-lock freezer bag and freeze for 6 months.

Nutrition per serving: Calories: 240 kcal; Fat: 10 g; Carbs: 10 g; Protein: 25 g

Zucchini Chews

Preparation time: 15 minutes

Cooking time: 6 hours

Servings: 10 chews

Ingredients:

- 2 tbsp olive oil
- 2 large zucchinis
- 2 tsp chicken bouillon
- 2 tsp dry mustard

Directions:

1. Cut the zucchini into slices about ⅛-inch thick.
2. Drizzle with olive oil and arrange them neatly on a cookie sheet.
3. Sprinkle the chicken bouillon and dry mustard over the zucchini slices.
4. Place them in the oven, then bake for 6 hours at 200°F.
5. Keep them in a sealed container for up to 2 weeks.

Nutrition per serving: Calories: 36 kcal; Fat: 2.8 g; Carbs: 2.2 g; Protein: 0.6 g

Sweet Turkey for Beginners

Preparation time: 30 minutes

Cooking time: 0 minutes

Servings: Approximately 27 lb

Ingredients:

- 6.6 lb turkey hearts and liver
- 11 lb turkey thighs, breasts, or tenderloins chopped into pieces
- 2.2 lb yams or sweet potatoes, finely chopped
- 2.2 lb cooked chickpeas1 cup dried eggs
- 2.2 lb cranberries
- 2.2 lb green beans

Directions:

1. Mix all ingredients until well combined.
2. Make portions and put them in separate bags or lunch boxes. Keep 1 bag in the refrigerator to use and the rest of the bags in the freezer.
3. Use within 2-3 weeks. Remove one bag from the freezer daily and place it in the refrigerator to thaw.
4. Serve at room temperature or warm.

Nutrition per serving: Calories: 500 kcal; Fat: 15 g; Carbs: 40 g; Protein: 45 g

Chicken Stew Homemade Dog Food

Preparation time: 45 minutes

Cooking time: 1 hour

Servings: 10 – 12 bags

Ingredients:

- 2 tbsp apple cider vinegar
- 4 eggs, hard-boiled
- 1 large whole chicken
- 1 cup celery, diced small
- 2 cups carrots, diced small
- 1 ½ cup water
- 2 cups white rice, cooked

Directions:

1. Add the chicken to a pot and boil for 1 hour. Do not discard the broth. When done, remove the chicken and shred it.
2. Boil the eggs and dice them.
3. Add the carrots, diced eggs, white rice, celery, vinegar, and chicken. Mix well.
4. Put one cup in one bag and store it.

Nutrition per serving: Calories: 200 kcal; Fat: 5 g; Carbs: 20 g; Protein: 15 g

Mixed Strawberry and Blueberry "Pupsicles"

Preparation time: 15 minutes

Cooking time: 0 minutes

Servings: Approximately 20 lb

Ingredients:

- 2 cups frozen strawberries
- 2 cups frozen blueberries
- 2 cups nonfat plain yogurt
- Water, as required
- ½ cup plain peanut butter

Directions:

1. Add all ingredients to a blender. Blend until smooth.
2. Pour into dog bone molds. You can also use ice trays.
3. Freeze until firm.
4. Remove from the mold and serve. Transfer the remaining popsicles into Ziploc bags and freeze them.

Nutrition per serving: Calories: 100 kcal; Fat: 1.5 g; Carbs: 13 g; Protein: 7 g

Meatloaf

Preparation time: 30 minutes

Cooking time: 1 hour 30 minutes

Servings: 1 meatloaf

Ingredients:

- ½ oz chopped parsley
- 4 oz peas
- 5 oz carrots, shredded
- 3 oz breadcrumbs, wheat, and gluten-free
- 1 lb beef, minced
- 2 tbsp tomato puree
- 4 oz parmesan cheese, low-fat
- 2 eggs, beaten

Directions:

1. Place the carrots and peas in a pot. Cook until soft.
2. Add the minced beef, Parmesan, breadcrumbs, parsley, puree, and eggs. Combine well.
3. Shape the mixture into meatloaf size. Place it gently on the pan.
4. Cover with lid and bake for 1 hour 30 minutes at 350°F.
5. Allow to cool, then cut and serve. Keep it in the refrigerator for up to a week.

Nutrition per serving: Calories: 1415 kcal; Fat: 78 g; Carbs: 59 g; Protein: 117 g

Chicken Liver Squares

Preparation time: 15 minutes

Cooking time: 2 hours

Servings: 50 squares

Ingredients:

- 1 lb chicken liver, rinsed
- 3 eggs
- 1 lb chicken

Directions:

1. Preheat your oven to 220°F. Place parchment paper on two cookie sheets.
2. Add the chicken to a food processor. Crack the eggs into the food processor and add the chicken liver. Purée the mixture.
3. Pour the mixture into the middle of the two cookie sheets. Place the sheets in the oven and bake for an hour. After that, cut each mixture into squares measuring 1 inch, then flip. Return the sheets to the oven and bake for an extra hour.
4. When the squares are browned, turn off the oven. Allow the cookie sheets to remain in the oven until they have completely cooled down.
5. Allow the squares to cool completely before serving or in the refrigerator. You can refrigerate it for 3 days or freeze it in a sealed container for up to 6 months.

Nutrition per serving: Calories: 40 kcal; Fat: 2 g; Carbs: 1 g; Protein: 4 g

Turkey and Greens for Beginners

Preparation time: 30 minutes

Cooking time: 0 minutes

Servings: Approximately 27 lb

Ingredients:

- 8 lb turkey thighs, breasts, or tenderloins chopped into pieces
- 3.3 lb ground turkey necks
- 6.6 lb turkey hearts and liver
- 2.2 lb turkey gizzard
- 2.2 lb lettuce, finely chopped
- 2.2 lb yams or sweet potatoes, finely chopped
- 2.2 lb zucchini, finely chopped

Directions:

1. Add turkey thighs or breasts or organ meat, gizzard, necks, lettuce, yam, or

sweet potato into a mixing bowl. Mix until well combined.

2. Make portions and place them in separate bags or lunch boxes. Keep 1 bag in the refrigerator to use and the rest of the bags in the freezer.
3. Use within 2-3 weeks. Remove one bag from the freezer daily and place it in the refrigerator to thaw.
4. Serve at room temperature or warm.

Nutrition per serving: Calories: 221 kcal; Fat: 11 g; Carbs: 18 g; Protein: 27 g

Deli Turkey Rollups

Preparation time: 20 minutes

Cooking time: 0 minutes

Servings: 30 treats

Ingredients:

- ¼ pound sliced low-sodium turkey breast
- 2 oz cream cheese

Directions:

1. Spread one or two tablespoons of cream cheese on a turkey breast slice.
2. Roll up tightly and slice into pieces about 1 inch in size.
3. Keep it in the refrigerator for a maximum of 3 days. To prevent them from unrolling, keep them flat in the freezer.

Nutrition per serving: Calories: 28 kcal; Fat: 1.6 g; Carbs: 0.6 g; Protein: 2.9 g

Rice and Yam Cakes

Preparation time: 30 minutes

Cooking time: 0 minutes

Servings: Approximately 24 lb

Ingredients:

- 4 cups brown or white rice
- 8 -10 cups water or unsalted chicken broth without onion
- 4 large yams, steamed or baked, mashed
- 4 cups pumpkin puree
- 1 lb green beans, finely chopped
- 1 lb snap peas
- 2 large parsley bunches, chopped
- 2 -3 dozen egg shells, baked in an oven until dry
- 18 eggs, lightly poached, cooled
- 2 cups natural peanut butter
- 1 ⅓ cup nutritional yeast
- 2 cups flax meal
- 2 cups raw pumpkin seeds or almonds, ground
- 2 cups rolled oats (optional)
- 2 cups rolled oats, ground (optional)
- 1 cup olive oil
- 1 cup rose hips, dried, ground in a coffee grinder
- 2 peaches, pitted, chopped
- 2 pears, cored, peeled, chopped
- 4 plums, pitted, chopped
- 8 large apples, cored, chopped
- 16 large carrots, finely chopped
- ½ head cabbage, finely chopped (do not grind)
- 2 heads broccoli, finely chopped
- 12 celery stalks, finely chopped
- 2 large zucchini or summer squash, finely chopped
- 1 lb cranberries
- 1 lb blueberries

Directions:

1. Add rice and broth into a saucepan or rice cooker and cook the rice.
2. Meanwhile, add the vegetables (except cabbage) or fruits that need to be finely chopped if desired in the food processor. Process until finely chopped.
3. Gather all the ingredients and add them to a mixing bowl. Mix until well combined.

4. Line 4-5 baking sheets with parchment paper. Make cakes of the mixture and place them on the baking sheet next to each other.
5. Place the baking trays in the freezer and freeze until firm.
6. Make portions and place them in separate bags or lunch boxes. Keep 1 bag in the refrigerator to use and the rest of the bags in the freezer.
7. Use within 2-3 weeks. Remove one bag from the freezer daily and place it in the refrigerator to thaw.
8. Serve at room temperature or warm.
9. Note: Some of the fruit or vegetables mentioned in the recipe may be seasonal, so you can substitute them for some other fruit or vegetable your dog prefers. You can also make changes suiting your dog's preference.

Nutrition per serving: Calories: 256 kcal; Fat: 5 g; Carbs: 8 g; Protein: 12 g

Beef Potato Carrot Stew

Preparation time: 5 minutes

Cooking time: 20 minutes

Servings: 4

Ingredients:

- 1 cup ground beef
- ½ cup carrots, cubed
- ½ cup potatoes, cubed
- ½ tsp cinnamon powder
- ¼ tsp turmeric
- ¼ tsp cumin powder
- ½ tsp sesame oil

Directions:

1. Heat the sesame oil In a pot.
2. Fry the ground beef for 3 minutes.
3. Add the potatoes and stir for 2 minutes.
4. Add the turmeric, cumin, and cinnamon. Stir for 2 minutes.

5. Add ½cupwater. Cook for 5 minutes.
6. Add the carrots, then cook for 5 minutes. Serve hot.

Nutrition per serving: Calories: 230 kcal; Fat: 12 g; Carbs: 12 g; Protein: 17 g

Chicken, Turkey, and Fish Delight

Preparation time: 25 minutes

Cooking time: 0 minutes

Servings: Approximately 25 lb

Ingredients:

- 1 1 lb herring, chopped into pieces
- 3.3 lb ground chicken bones and turkey bones
- 6.6 lb chicken and turkey hearts and liver
- 2.2 lb cooked chickpeas
- 2.2 lb spinach, finely chopped
- 3 chicken eggs, lightly boiled

Directions:

1. Add all ingredients into a mixing bowl. Mix until well combined.
2. Make portions and place them in separate bags or lunch boxes. Keep 1 bag in the refrigerator to use and the rest of the bags in the freezer.
3. Use within 2-3 weeks. Remove one bag from the freezer daily and place it in the refrigerator to thaw.
4. Serve at room temperature or warm.

Nutrition per serving: Calories: 241 kcal; Fat: 14 g; Carbs: 7 g; Protein: 16 g

Berry Yoghurt Treats

Preparation time: 15 minutes

Cooking time: 0 minutes

Servings: Approximately 22 lb

Ingredients:

- ½ cup plain yogurt
- ½ cup fresh or frozen strawberries
- ½ cup fresh or frozen blueberries

Directions:

1. Using a food blender, blitz all ingredients until smooth.
2. Pour into ice cube trays or popsicle molds and place it in the freezer for 2-3 hours or until solid.

Nutrition per serving: Calories: 10 kcal; Fat: 0.1 g; Carbs: 1.6 g; Protein: 0.6 g

Banana and Wheat Germ Balls

Preparation time: 20 minutes

Cooking time: 0 minutes

Servings: Approximately 10/12 servings

Ingredients:

- ¼ cup unsalted peanuts chopped
- ¼ cup wheat germ
- ½ cup peanut butter
- 1 ripe banana

Directions:

1. Mash the banana and peanut butter in a small bowl using a fork.
2. Add the wheat germ and mix well.
3. Place it in the refrigerator for about an hour until firm.
4. With your hands, roll a rounded teaspoon of mixture into balls.
5. Roll balls in peanuts, coating them evenly.
6. Place them on a cookie sheet in the freezer.
7. When completely frozen, pack into air-tight containers and refrigerate.

Nutrition per serving: Calories: 13 kcal; Fat: 1 g; Carbs: 1 g; Protein: 4 g

Banana Pumpkin Dog Pops

Preparation time: 15 minutes

Cooking time: 0 minutes

Servings: Approximately 22 lb

Ingredients:

- 1 ripe banana, peeled
- 1 cup plain yogurt, non-fat
- 15 oz pumpkin puree
- 1 tsp organic honey

Directions:

1. Place the peeled banana and pumpkin puree into a food processor. Pulse until the mixture is smooth. Transfer the mixture to a mixing bowl.
2. Add the yogurt to the banana mixture and mix until well combined. Stir in the honey.
3. Press the mixture into the desired molds and set it in the freezer. Freeze overnight.
4. Pop the frozen treats out of the mold and into an airtight container. Store in the freezer until ready to use.

Nutrition per serving: Calories: 21 kcal; Fat: 0.1 g; Carbs: 4.3 g; Protein: 0.9 g

Homemade Grain-Free Allergy Treats

Preparation time: 10 minutes

Cooking time: 25 minutes

Servings: 24 treats

Ingredients:

- 1 cup water
- ½ banana, mashed
- 1 ¼ cup coconut flour
- ½ cup pumpkin
- ½ cup unsweetened applesauce

- 2 carrots, grated

Directions:

1. Pour the flour into a bowl. Add the water, banana, carrots, applesauce, and pumpkin. Combine well.
2. Form the mixture into small balls. Place them on a cookie sheet and flatten them.
3. Place them in the oven, then bake for 20-25 minutes at 350°F. Allow to cool completely before serving.
4. Keep them in a sealed container in the refrigerator.

Nutrition per serving: Calories: 36 kcal; Fat: 1.5 g; Carbs: 5 g; Protein: 1 g

Beef with Mushroom, Carrot, and Pomegranate

Preparation time: 5 minutes

Cooking time: 20 minutes

Servings: 4

Ingredients:

- 2 carrots, cubed
- ½ cup spinach, chopped
- 2 radishes, shredded
- ½ cup pomegranate seeds
- 1 cup ground beef
- 2 tbsp leek, chopped
- ¼ cup beef broth
- 1 tsp cumin
- ½ tsp turmeric
- ½ tsp cinnamon
- ⅓ cup mushroom, chopped
- 10 basil leaves, chopped
- 1 tsp olive oil

Directions:

1. In a big pot, heat the olive oil.
2. Fry the ground beef until brown.
3. Add the leek, carrot, radish, and mushroom.

4. Stir for 3 minutes. Add cinnamon, turmeric, cumin and stir for 2 minutes.
5. Add the spinach, basil leaves and stir for 1 minute.
6. Add the beef broth and cook for 2 minutes.
7. Let it cool down. Add the pomegranate seeds. Mix and then serve.

Nutrition per serving: Calories: 250 kcal; Fat: 15 g; Carbs: 12 g; Protein: 18 g

Pumpkin Purée

Preparation time: 10 minutes

Cooking time: 35 minutes

Servings: 2-4 cups

Ingredients:

- Water, as needed
- 1 small cooking pumpkin

Directions:

1. Preheat your oven to 350°F. Using parchment paper, line a cookie sheet.
2. Wash the pumpkin under running water. Cut off the top and remove the seeds from the pumpkin using a spoon. Cut the unseeded pumpkin into quarters.
3. Arrange the quarters neatly on a baking sheet. Bake in the oven for 30-35 minutes.
4. Retrieve them from the oven and allow them to cool. Peel off the baked pumpkin skin and discard it.
5. Chop the pumpkin into cubes, then transfer them into a food processor. Add water as needed to puree it.
6. Store it in a sealed container in the freezer for up to 6 months.

Nutrition per serving: Calories: 50 kcal; Fat: 1 g; Carbs: 10 g; Protein: 1 g

Slow-Cooked Chicken

Preparation time: 10 minutes

Cooking time: 12 hours

Servings: About 9 cups

Ingredients:

- Water, as needed
- 3 boneless, skinless chicken breasts
- 1 cup uncooked brown rice
- 1 sweet potato, cubed (unpeeled but with any green parts removed)
- 2 carrots, cut into 1 round
- ½ cup cranberries

Directions:

1. Place all the ingredients in a 4-quart slow cooker. Add water as needed.
2. Cook on low heat overnight, about 12 hours.
3. Allow the meal to cool before serving. Keep it in the refrigerator for three days, or freeze it in a sealed container for six months, based on your preference.

Nutrition per serving: Calories: 280 kcal; Fat: 3 g; Carbs: 44 g; Protein: 20 g

Terrier's Beef Fried Rice

Preparation time: 8 minutes

Cooking time: 35 minutes

Servings: 7 cups

Ingredients:

- 1 tbsp sesame oil
- ½ cup frozen carrots and peas, chopped
- 2 cups water
- 1 cup uncooked jasmine rice
- ½ cup soy sauce
- ½ cup celery, chopped
- 2 eggs
- 1 lb lean ground beef

Directions:

1. In a pan over high heat, bring your water to a boil. Once the water is boiling, add the rice and stir. Return your water to a boil, then lower the heat and cover. Then, simmer until your rice is tender and your water has been absorbed. It should take about 25 minutes—fluff the rice with a fork and then set it aside.
2. Spray a skillet with some nonstick cooking spray and heat over a medium-high fire.
3. Beat the eggs in a small bowl, pour them into the skillet, and cook until firm.
4. Remove the eggs from the heat and slice them into strips. Mix the eggs with the rice and set it aside.
5. Respray the skillet with some nonstick cooking spray and place it over medium-high heat.
6. Add the ground beef and celery to the skillet and cook for about 10 minutes or until the beef is thoroughly cooked.
7. Mix the soy sauce and sesame oil in a bowl, then pour over the beef mixture. Add the carrots, peas, cooked eggs, and cooked rice, then stir and cook for 4 minutes.
8. Completely cool before serving, keep in your fridge for up to 3 days, or freeze in an airtight container for up to 3 months.

Nutrition per serving: Calories: 375 kcal; Fat: 14 g; Carbs: 36 g; Protein: 25 g

Shopping List

Meat and Protein:

- Chicken (whole, boneless, or ground)
- Beef (ground or stew meat)
- Turkey (ground or lean cuts)
- Salmon (fresh or canned)
- Liver (chicken or beef)

Vegetables:

- Cauliflower
- Carrots
- Squash (such as zucchini or butternut squash)
- Mushrooms
- Spinach
- Broccoli
- Sweet potatoes
- Beetroot
- Green beans
- Corn
- Kale

Fruits:

- Bananas
- Apples
- Mango
- Pear
- Blueberries
- Strawberries
- Watermelon
- Kiwi

Grains and Carbohydrates:

- Rice (brown or white)
- Oats
- Couscous
- Potatoes

- Lentils
- Chickpeas
- Oatmeal
- Wheat germ

Dairy and Eggs:

- Yogurt (plain, non-fat)
- Eggs

Healthy Fats and Oils:

- Peanut butter
- Almond butter
- Olive oil
- Canola oil
- Cod liver oil
- Flaxseed oil

Herbs and Spices:

- Basil
- Parsley
- Cilantro
- Turmeric

Others:

- Biscuits (for banana biscuits)
- Kidney beans
- Pomegranate
- Cheese
- Muffin ingredients (for sausage, spinach cheese muffins)
- Almonds (for almond banana dog treat)
- Honey (optional for some treat recipes)
- Molasses (optional for some treat recipes)

Conclusion

Now you've got all the information you need to give your dog the food its body needs most. That's the sign of an incredibly loving and dedicated pet parent. Your dog might not be able to say in words how much it will appreciate your actions, but it will let you know at mealtime!

Thank you for reading our book, and we hope you will try homemade cooking for your dog so you can have a healthy, happy dog with an excellent quality of life for many years to come.

Enjoy cooking for your pup and "Bon Appetit"!

Congratulations on reaching the end of "Home Made Healthy Dog Food Cookbook!" I hope you have found this culinary adventure for your furry companion rewarding and enjoyable. Now that you have equipped yourself with the knowledge and recipes to create nutritious meals for your dog, I would love to hear about your experience.

Has this cookbook inspired you to become a dog chef extraordinaire? Or have you discovered a recipe that has become your pup's favorite? I would love it if you would share your experience with me and other dog lovers by leaving a review.

Your feedback is important to me, and it will help other readers confidently embark on the journey to homemade dog food.

Lucy Irving

Index

Rice and Yam Cakes; 74

Rover's Deviled Eggs; 56

Rover's Raw Chicken Dinner; 62

Salmon and Spinach Hash; 65

Salmon and Vegetables Meatballs; 47

Sausage Spinach Cheese Muffins; 47

Slow-Cooked Chicken; 78

Spinach Omelet; 43

Squash With Chicken And Basil; 25

Strawberry and Kiwi Yogurt Treats; 44

Super Nutritious Dog Bowl; 54

Sweet Potato Potstickers; 70

Sweet Turkey for Beginners; 72

Terrier Chicken Meatloaf; 41

Terrier's Beef Fried Rice; 78

Tuna Casserole; 35

Turkey and Greens for Beginners; 73

Turkey Carrot Spinach and Corn; 55

Turkey Fried Rice; 56

Turkey Gravy; 58

Turkey Oatmeal Doggy Biscuits; 34

Vegan Homemade Dog Food; 45

Vegetable and Minced Meat Dog Food; 48

Wallace's Spinach Sprats; 40

Yogurt and Watermelon Frozen Treats; 33

Yummy Homemade Meat Cakes; 35

Zoe's Buffalo Meatballs; 48

Zucchini Chews; 71

Printed in Great Britain
by Amazon